GENOA

TRAVEL GUIDE 2025-2026

Comprehensive Handbook To 40 Must-See Attractions And Memorable Experiences For Tourists

ANTHONY LAFRENIERE

Gratitude

To everyone holding this guide in your hands or scrolling through its pages, thank you. Your curiosity, passion for travel, and trust in my work mean the world to me. Creating this guide to Genoa has been a journey in itself, shaped not only by my explorations but by countless conversations with fellow travelers, stories shared over espresso in tucked-away piazzas, and the joy of discovering hidden corners of this remarkable city.

Whether you're a first-time visitor or a seasoned explorer of Italy, I hope this guide adds value to your adventure, sparks your curiosity, and helps you build lasting memories in Genoa. Your support, through reading, sharing, and recommending this book, enables me to continue doing what I love: making travel accessible, immersive, and personal.

As a token of appreciation, I've included something special for you: a Bonus Itinerary Planner Template. It's designed to help you organize your trip both within Genoa and beyond, making your travel planning more intentional and enjoyable.

To access your bonus, scroll through the bonus section carefully placed within this book. I wanted this to be a true gift for readers, something exclusive and thoughtfully tucked away, waiting for you once you've joined me fully on this journey.

With all my gratitude and a wish for safe, inspired travels,
Anthony Lafreniere.

How To Use This Book

This guide has been thoughtfully designed to help you explore Genoa with confidence, curiosity, and clarity. Each chapter provides detailed information, curated recommendations, and locally inspired insights to ensure your travel experience is as smooth and enriching as possible.

However, it's important to understand that some elements, particularly related to schedules, accessibility, and certain attractions, can change between the time of writing and your actual date of travel. In order to avoid outdated or inaccurate details, I've chosen not to include sensitive time-based information that is likely to change.

Instead, I've embedded Google Map links in the form of QR codes throughout the guide. These QR codes provide up-to-date directions and details for attractions, helping you stay current with the latest updates, entrance times, and even temporary closures or reroutes.

Here's how to use them:

- For Paperback Readers: Simply open your phone's camera, hold it steadily over the QR code, and click the notification that appears. It will redirect you to the exact location or listing on Google Maps.
- For Kindle or Digital Readers: Take a screenshot of the QR code you wish to scan. Then open Google Lens (available in the Google app), upload the screenshot, and you'll be given the option to open the embedded link for full details and directions.

For attractions or activities that do not include a QR code, I recommend copying the name and performing a quick search online. This allows you to access the most recent updates, including seasonal schedules, booking requirements, or special event notices.

Using this approach allows the book to stay relevant longer and ensures you always have access to the most accurate, real-time information, no matter when or where you're reading it.

Happy exploring!

Contents

ABOUT THE AUTHOR

Anthony Lafreniere is an experienced travel writer and adventurer who is passionate about finding the hidden treasures of unusual places. With a lifetime devoted to discovering various cultures and landscapes, Anthony has written a number of travel guides that let readers experience the essence of each destination by fusing insightful commentary with captivating storytelling. His writing reflects his profound understanding of history, regional customs, and the beauty of nature, which makes his guides enlightening and motivational.

Anthony is well-known for his meticulousness and ability to engage with locals. His writings offer more than just travel plans; they give readers a greater comprehension of the residents, landmarks, and histories that influence each place. His trips are enhanced with thought-provoking discussions, historical site visits, and a dedication to advancing eco-friendly travel.

Anthony likes to do historical study and plot his next trip when he's not writing or discovering new places. His guides are now dependable travel companions for tourists looking for unique and unforgettable encounters outside the usual route.

INTRODUCTION

The first time I stepped foot in Genoa, I arrived on a stormy spring afternoon, my suitcase wheels rattling over ancient cobblestones slick with rain. I had taken a detour from a planned trip to Florence, urged by an old friend, a travel photographer, who once described Genoa as *"the city that speaks in whispers."* He was right. Genoa doesn't shout its beauty the way Venice does or show off like Rome. Instead, it rewards the curious: those who linger in its narrow alleys, who look up at fading frescoes, who listen to church bells echoing between the stone facades.

That first visit was unplanned, and yet it became unforgettable.

Since then, I've returned to Genoa four more times, each with different people and for different reasons: once with a couple exploring Italy on their honeymoon; once with an architecture student tracing the legacy of Renzo Piano; another time with a group of solo travelers trying to escape the crowds of Cinque Terre; and most recently, with an older woman named Mireille who had last been to Genoa in the 1970s and wanted to revisit the Aquarium she helped fund in her youth.

Each trip revealed a new layer of the city, and more importantly, revealed how much travelers overlook or underestimate this coastal gem.

This guide was born from those experiences.

Over the past decade, I've written and contributed to dozens of travel handbooks. Some have focused on major capital cities; others on overlooked coastal towns or remote mountain villages. But my favorite guides, the ones that seem to resonate most with readers, are the ones that don't just list what to do, but invite you to connect with a place on a deeper level.

Genoa demands that kind of connection.

It's not a city that gives itself up easily. You won't find sweeping piazzas crowded with tour groups or souvenir shops every few feet. Instead, you'll find a maze of medieval streets called "caruggi," home to both history and surprise. You'll follow a seemingly ordinary alley only to emerge in a sunlit square where locals sip espresso beside faded marble statues. You'll stumble upon a frescoed palace that's now a museum, one you've never heard of, but will never forget.

What makes Genoa different from so many Italian destinations is this layered complexity. It's a port city, an aristocratic city, a working-class city, a place of past glory and present innovation. And because of that, it's a dream for thoughtful, curious travelers, like yourself.

The year 2025–2026 is a particularly exciting time to visit Genoa. A surge in investment and tourism development has brought fresh energy to the old city. The city's innovative Smart Tourism initiatives have transformed it into one of Europe's rising cultural hubs. From the revitalized Porto Antico district, now pulsing with life, dining, and art, to the award-winning Galata Museo del Mare, Genoa is redefining what it means to blend the historic with the modern.

The Palazzi dei Rolli, once elite family homes, have never been more accessible or better curated. And the Genovese food scene? Let's just say this isn't just the birthplace of pesto. It's a city where focaccia is practically a religion, where street food vendors still pass down their stalls across generations, and where a meal often turns into a memory.

Yet despite all this, Genoa remains underrated, and that's precisely what makes it so special. It hasn't been polished for mass tourism. It's authentic, evolving, and incredibly real.

While writing this guide, I revisited Genoa with a simple mission: to explore it from the point of view of travelers at every stage, first-timers, history lovers, culinary adventurers, couples, families, and solo wanderers. I stayed in both boutique hotels and budget B&Bs. I took funiculars to hilltop forts and wandered back down on foot, talking to locals, shopkeepers, artists, and guides.

I met Matteo, a retired sailor who now leads storytelling tours in the old harbor. I met Céline, a backpacker from Québec who arrived for two days and stayed for three weeks, working remotely from a hidden café above Piazza delle Erbe. And I met a young Nigerian-Italian musician named Leko who gave me one of the most insightful perspectives on Genoa's multicultural rhythm, something most tourists never hear about.

These people, and so many more, helped shape the spirit of this guide. You'll find not just places, but the stories behind them.

Of course, you'll find curated recommendations: 40 must-see attractions, covering palaces, cathedrals, museums, fortresses, food markets, sea-facing marvels, and hidden gems. But I didn't stop at just listing addresses and opening times.

As said earlier in the previous section, I've included carefully embedded QR codes that link directly to Google Maps directions. That way, you can quickly navigate your journey while avoiding outdated printed information.

This choice was deliberate.

You may be reading this guide weeks before your trip, or perhaps you're sitting at a Genoese café as we speak, espresso in hand, guide open on your lap. However, you've arrived here, know that you are not alone. You're part of a community of travelers who value authenticity, respect local culture, and seek more than just another selfie spot.

This book is not about checking off boxes, it's about immersing yourself in a city with a soul. It's about that moment when you turn a corner and see the sea stretch out in front of you, golden in the sunset. It's about the stories carved into stone facades, the scent of basil in the air, and the soft sound of Italian conversations carried on a breeze.

Welcome to Genoa.

Let's begin.

CHAPTER 1: INTRODUCING GENOA, ITALY

A Brief Overview of Genoa's Growth and Modern Development

Genoa, or Genova in Italian, stands as a city of transformation. Once the powerful capital of a maritime republic, it has grown, adapted, and redefined itself repeatedly across centuries. Today, Genoa is a dynamic city that blends historical grandeur with contemporary innovation, earning recognition as one of Italy's most intriguing and forward-thinking urban destinations.

Nestled between the Ligurian Sea and the Apennine Mountains, Genoa's growth has always been tied to its strategic geographic location. As Italy's busiest port and one of the largest in Europe, Genoa has long played a critical role in Mediterranean trade. Yet in recent decades, its economy, infrastructure, tourism, and urban identity have evolved in remarkable ways that make it a city of not only the past but also of the future.

Genoa's development was once synonymous with sea power. During the 11th to 15th centuries, the Republic of Genoa dominated maritime trade routes across the Mediterranean and Black Sea. It amassed immense wealth and political clout rivaling Venice and Pisa, while Genoese bankers and merchants extended their influence deep into Europe and the Middle East.

However, Genoa's dominance declined gradually with the rise of other European powers, and by the 18th century, its political independence had faded. Fast-forward to the 19th and 20th centuries, and Genoa reinvented itself as an industrial hub, specializing in shipbuilding, steel, and transportation. Massive docks and shipyards transformed the port area into the heartbeat of Italy's industrial economy.

By the 1980s, however, like many Western industrial cities, Genoa faced economic stagnation. Shipbuilding declined, industrial jobs diminished, and the city had to address challenges related to urban decay, pollution, and declining infrastructure. Yet this difficult period became a turning point, spurring Genoa's pivot from heavy industry to a diversified, modern economy that embraced technology, tourism, culture, and sustainability.

Genoa's comeback has been particularly visible in its urban planning and infrastructure projects. Since the 1990s, the city has invested heavily in regenerating its historic center and neglected industrial zones, bringing them back to life with new public spaces, cultural institutions, and transport systems.

A cornerstone of this transformation was the 1992 Expo celebrating the 500th anniversary of Christopher Columbus's voyage. To prepare, Genoa undertook a massive redevelopment of the Porto Antico (Old Port) under the design of famed architect Renzo Piano. This revitalized waterfront is now one of the city's most beloved destinations, home to the Aquarium of Genoa (one of Europe's largest), the Bigo panoramic lift, museums, restaurants, marinas, and family-friendly attractions.

In addition to revitalizing tourist areas, Genoa has expanded its public transport network with significant investments in its metro, elevators, funiculars, and buses. A push for "vertical mobility", integrating hilltop neighborhoods into the city using innovative lifts and cable cars, makes Genoa one of Europe's most walkable and accessible cities, despite its rugged terrain.

Major new projects continue shaping the city. The Parco del Ponte area, built on the site of the collapsed Morandi Bridge, showcases Genoa's resilience and rebirth, centered around the new San Giorgio Bridge designed by Renzo Piano. Meanwhile, the Erzelli Great Campus, a modern hilltop tech park, is attracting innovation and research initiatives, aligning Genoa with the high-tech economy of the future.

In recent years, Genoa has embraced the green city model, aiming to balance economic growth with environmental sustainability. The city has implemented policies to reduce traffic congestion and pollution while promoting eco-mobility. Notably, Genoa's public transport, including metro trains, elevators, and buses, has been made free for residents and visitors under various initiatives in 2024–2025. This bold move encourages the use of sustainable transport and has become a model other Italian cities are watching closely.

The city is also pursuing the creation of more green spaces, repurposed urban areas, and walkable streets. The Levante Waterfront, again led by Renzo Piano's studio, continues to evolve with a focus on accessibility, landscaping, and leisure zones.

Digital transformation is another key to Genoa's development. The city's VisitGenoa app and virtual reality tools help tourists navigate and explore attractions in an interactive, sustainable way. Genoa's push for smart tourism and accessibility has made it a 2025 finalist for the European Capital of Smart Tourism award, highlighting its strides in innovation, sustainability, and inclusive development.

While Genoa once thrived on industrial might, today it thrives on culture, education, and tourism. The city has smartly leveraged its historical sites, museums, and festivals to attract international visitors and cruise travelers.

Its old town, Centro Storico di Genova, is one of the largest medieval city centers in Europe, recognized as a UNESCO World Heritage Site. The narrow alleyways known as caruggi, ancient palaces along Via Garibaldi, and ornate churches have become key draws for culture-seeking tourists.

Museums such as the Galata Museo del Mare, Palazzo Reale, and Castello d'Albertis showcase Genoa's artistic and maritime legacy, while new venues host contemporary art, music, and film events. The Carlo Felice Theatre and local music festivals breathe modern life into Genoa's creative scene.

At the same time, the city has built a reputation as a culinary destination. Genoese pesto, focaccia, seafood, and fine Ligurian wines make dining in Genoa a full experience. With new boutique hotels, upscale stays, and improved cruise facilities, Genoa's tourism infrastructure is more sophisticated than ever before.

As of 2025, Genoa is more than a historical port city, it is a vibrant, livable, and future-oriented destination. Its blend of maritime tradition and urban innovation places it among Italy's most underrated yet rewarding cities for travelers.

Efforts to connect Genoa more effectively to national and European networks are also accelerating. The upcoming Tortona, Genoa high-speed rail link, expected by 2026, will shorten travel times to Milan and northern Europe significantly. The city's airport, Cristoforo Colombo, is being integrated with a new railway station and mobility center at Erzelli, allowing for seamless airport-to-city connections.

Moreover, Genoa is capitalizing on its position along the Italian Riviera to create integrated tourism routes with nearby Cinque Terre, Portofino, and Savona. These efforts ensure that Genoa isn't just a standalone city but a gateway to the broader Ligurian experience.

Genoa's growth and modern development story is one of resilience, reinvention, and regeneration. From its ancient roots as a seafaring power to its current status as a smart, sustainable, and culturally rich metropolis, Genoa is living proof that cities can evolve while preserving their soul.

Whether you're visiting for its historic landmarks, flavorful cuisine, scenic coastlines, or tech-forward innovations, Genoa in 2025–2026 offers something genuinely unique: a seamless blend of old and new, tradition and transformation.

Why Genoa Is a Must-See Destination for Any Traveler

With its unique blend of maritime history, grand Renaissance architecture, authentic Italian lifestyle, and cutting-edge cultural renewal, Genoa offers a rich and layered travel experience that rivals more famous Italian destinations, yet feels far less commercialized. Whether you're a first-time visitor to Italy or a seasoned explorer looking for something off the usual tourist path, Genoa presents a compelling case as a must-see destination for any traveler in 2025 and beyond.

A City of Rich Historical Significance

Genoa's story spans over two millennia, and its influence during the medieval and Renaissance periods shaped global trade, politics, and maritime navigation. As one of the powerful Maritime Republics alongside Venice, Pisa, and Amalfi, Genoa rose to dominance through seafaring prowess and commercial ingenuity. It was the birthplace of the great explorer Christopher Columbus and once served as a central hub in Mediterranean commerce.

Today, the legacy of Genoa's golden era can still be seen in the stunning Strade Nuove (New Streets) and Palazzi dei Rolli, a collection of grand Renaissance and Baroque palaces that line Via Garibaldi. Recognized as a UNESCO World Heritage Site, this historic district immerses visitors in a world of gilded ceilings, sweeping marble staircases, and opulent salons that once hosted ambassadors, princes, and emperors. This living history makes Genoa a paradise for lovers of European heritage and culture.

An Authentic Italian Experience, Without the Crowds

One of Genoa's most charming features is its authenticity. Unlike Venice or Florence, which have become overwhelmed by mass tourism, Genoa has preserved a genuine, lived-in feel. It's a city where local life unfolds naturally in the vibrant alleyways (called caruggi), where nonnas shop for produce at open-air markets, and where fishermen still dock their boats at Porto Antico. For travelers seeking a more intimate and unfiltered version of Italy, Genoa delivers in spades.

This authenticity extends to the city's culinary scene, which is delightfully rooted in regional traditions. Ligurian cuisine, with its focus on fresh seafood, aromatic herbs, and olive oil, offers a flavorful departure from heavier Italian dishes found elsewhere. From the world-famous pesto alla genovese to freshly baked focaccia dripping in olive oil, Genoa is a food lover's dream. And unlike in major tourist cities, meals are often affordably priced and prepared with seasonal, locally sourced ingredients.

A Living Canvas of Architecture and Art

Architecturally, Genoa is a visual marvel. The cityscape is an eclectic fusion of medieval towers, Baroque palazzi, Neoclassical churches, and 19th-century mansions clinging to the hillsides. The historic core is one of the largest in Europe, offering a seemingly endless labyrinth of cobbled streets, secret courtyards, and ancient chapels.

Cultural institutions like Palazzo Reale, Galata Museo del Mare, and Palazzo Ducale house masterpieces of Italian art, rare maritime relics, and international exhibitions. In recent years, modernity has also made its mark. Renzo Piano, the acclaimed Genoese architect behind the Centre Pompidou in Paris, helped revitalize the Porto Antico area, transforming the once-neglected harbor into a thriving cultural and recreational zone. The Aquarium of Genoa, one of the largest in Europe, stands as a testament to this modern regeneration.

Whether admiring a Caravaggio painting, attending a classical concert at Teatro Carlo Felice, or gazing up at medieval frescoes in a tiny chapel, Genoa invites travelers to explore the relationship between art, history, and daily life in a way that feels tangible and alive.

Stunning Natural Backdrop and Scenic Coastline

Nestled between the mountains and the Ligurian Sea, Genoa boasts one of the most picturesque urban landscapes in Italy. The city's dramatic topography, with buildings terraced into the hills and panoramic belvederes overlooking the Mediterranean, creates endless opportunities for scenic strolls, hikes, and unforgettable photo moments.

From Spianata Castelletto's sweeping views of red rooftops and church domes to sunset over the Boccadasse fishing village, Genoa serves up spectacular vistas without ever needing to leave the city. And for those eager to explore beyond, the famed Ligurian Riviera, including Camogli, Santa Margherita Ligure, and Portofino, is just a short train or boat ride away.

Travelers seeking a balance between urban discovery and natural beauty will find that Genoa offers the best of both worlds. Beaches, gardens, and nature reserves like Parco del Peralto are never far, allowing for a truly diverse travel experience.

Gateway to the Italian Riviera and Beyond

Another reason why Genoa is a must-visit destination is its strategic location. As the capital of Liguria, Genoa serves as the gateway to one of the most enchanting coastal regions in Europe, the Italian Riviera. From here, visitors can easily reach the colorful cliffside villages of Cinque Terre, the chic resorts of Portofino, or the alpine charm of the Ligurian hinterlands.

Genoa's well-connected transportation system, including regional trains, ferries, and an international airport, makes it an ideal base for both short and extended explorations across northern Italy. Whether you're planning a multi-city Italian itinerary or seeking a single-city stay with diverse day-trip options, Genoa's accessibility is a huge advantage.

A Forward-Looking, Smart City

As Genoa looks toward the future, it continues to embrace innovation and sustainability in tourism. The city has been recognized as a finalist for the 2025 European Capital of Smart Tourism, thanks to its digital city tools, free public transit for residents and visitors, and initiatives promoting eco-friendly travel.

The Genoa City Pass, integrated with apps for navigation and attraction access, is designed to simplify the travel experience. Meanwhile, the ongoing redevelopment of the Levante Waterfront, once again under the guidance of Renzo Piano, aims to create an inclusive, green, and technologically advanced urban space.

For 21st-century travelers who value sustainability, digital convenience, and thoughtful infrastructure, Genoa is emerging as one of Italy's most forward-thinking cities.

A City That Surprises and Delights

Perhaps the most compelling reason to visit Genoa is the element of surprise. Many travelers come expecting a gritty port city—and leave in awe of its beauty, history, and heart. Genoa doesn't try to impress with postcard-perfect clichés; instead, it quietly unfolds, revealing its soul through every detail: the aroma of espresso wafting from a centuries-old café, the glint of mosaics in a forgotten church, or the laughter of children playing in a hillside piazza.

It's a city for curious wanderers, art enthusiasts, culinary adventurers, and cultural explorers alike. Genoa rewards those who linger, who explore its alleyways with open eyes and minds, who engage with locals, and who allow the city to reveal itself gradually.

As travel trends continue to shift toward authenticity, sustainability, and immersive cultural experiences, Genoa stands out as a destination that checks every box. It is not just a stopover or a port of call, it is a city worthy of your time, attention, and admiration.

For the traveler seeking more than just iconic snapshots, for the traveler who craves story, substance, and surprise, Genoa is not only a must-see destination; it is a must-feel experience.

CHAPTER 2: HISTORY AND CULTURE OF GENOA

From Maritime Republic to Modern Port City

Genoa's transformation from a powerful maritime republic to a thriving modern port city is a captivating tale of resilience, reinvention, and deep-rooted cultural pride. Its rich history, shaped by waves of conquest, seafaring trade, political maneuvering, and industrial innovation, continues to echo through its elegant palaces, bustling waterfronts, narrow medieval alleyways, and vibrant urban culture.

Genoa's maritime legacy began to take shape in the early Middle Ages. Although the area had been inhabited since pre-Roman times and saw development under Roman rule as Genua, the city's identity as a naval and commercial powerhouse came into focus around the 11th century. As feudalism began to wane across Italy, Genoa established itself as a self-governing commune, eventually rising to prominence as one of the four great Maritime Republics of Italy, alongside Venice, Pisa, and Amalfi.

From the 11th to the 15th century, Genoa was at the height of its naval and trading dominance. Its fleet ruled over key trade routes in the Mediterranean and Black Seas, and Genoese merchants established commercial outposts as far afield as Constantinople, Crimea, North Africa, and the Levant. The city's prosperity was built on trade in spices, silk, grain, and precious metals, but also banking, shipbuilding, and, controversially, its involvement in the slave trade.

Genoa's aristocracy grew wealthy and influential. Rivalries with other maritime republics were common, particularly with Pisa and Venice, resulting in a series of naval battles for dominance. Genoa defeated Pisa in the Battle of Meloria (1284), securing control of the Tyrrhenian Sea. However, its conflict with Venice culminated in the Battle of Chioggia (1380), where Genoa's naval power began to wane following a major defeat.

Despite political turmoil and military losses, Genoa remained a wealthy and strategically important city. During its golden age in the 16th century, it became a hub of Renaissance finance and art, thanks largely to a powerful banking class and alliances with Spain's Habsburg monarchy.

One of Genoa's most famous sons is Christopher Columbus, born in the city in 1451. His voyages, backed by the Spanish crown, would usher in the age of European exploration and colonization. While Columbus is a complex and controversial figure today, his birthplace remains a site of interest for visitors and a symbol of Genoa's global connections.

The wealth generated during Genoa's powerful centuries helped shape its urban beauty. The aristocracy commissioned elegant palaces, particularly along Via Garibaldi (formerly Strada Nuova). These magnificent Renaissance and Baroque residences, many of which now function as museums, galleries, and civic buildings, are part of the UNESCO-listed Palazzi dei Rolli, a system of noble homes used to host state guests. Their ornate façades and lavish interiors tell the story of a city that once sat at the pinnacle of Mediterranean influence.

By the 17th and 18th centuries, Genoa's influence began to decline. Shifting trade routes, especially those favoring the Atlantic world over the Mediterranean, reduced the city's commercial importance. Plagues, economic challenges, and internal aristocratic divisions further weakened Genoa.

The city was eventually occupied by Napoleon in 1797. The once-mighty Republic of Genoa was dissolved and transformed into the Ligurian Republic, a satellite state under French control. It was formally annexed into the Kingdom of Sardinia in 1815, signaling the end of Genoa's independence.

Despite the loss of its republican status, Genoa remained economically and politically significant in northern Italy. The 19th century saw Genoa playing a pivotal role in the Risorgimento, the movement for Italian unification. The city was a key center of revolutionary thought, and the Ligurian coast was the birthplace of many nationalist leaders and intellectuals.

By the late 19th and early 20th centuries, Genoa had reinvented itself as a major industrial hub. Its port, already historically important, became a central cog in Italy's modern shipping, shipbuilding, and steel industries. The city's workers became central players in labor movements, while the port handled increasing volumes of commercial cargo.

During World War II, Genoa was heavily bombed due to its strategic importance. Much of the historic center and the port district suffered damage. However, post-war reconstruction brought modernization while preserving key historical sites. Genoa was rebuilt with a renewed focus on maritime trade, logistics, and industrial innovation.

In the decades following the war, Genoa's port became one of the busiest in Europe. Today, the Port of Genoa is Italy's largest seaport, facilitating both cargo and passenger movement across the Mediterranean and beyond. It's a key gateway for cruise ships and a logistical hub for industries ranging from textiles to technology.

In recent decades, Genoa has sought to reconnect with its artistic and architectural past while embracing the future. A key moment came in 2004 when Genoa was designated the European Capital of Culture. This led to major revitalization projects, including the redevelopment of Porto Antico (the old harbor), designed by world-renowned architect Renzo Piano, a native of the city.

This waterfront area now features world-class attractions such as the Aquarium of Genoa, the Biosfera, the Bigo panoramic elevator, and a variety of shops, museums, and restaurants. What was once a crumbling industrial zone is now a vibrant space for both locals and tourists, symbolizing Genoa's ability to reimagine itself while preserving its identity.

Genoa has also embraced its heritage as a city of culture and knowledge. Its historic libraries, museums, and universities continue to serve as centers for research, innovation, and artistic expression. New digital initiatives, such as smart tourism tools and interactive museum experiences, signal a forward-looking approach to heritage preservation.

Today's Genoa is a blend of old-world charm and contemporary dynamism. The medieval streets of the "caruggi", the monumental churches, the Renaissance palaces, and the lively local markets coexist with cutting-edge shipping logistics, international business, and cultural events.

The city's ability to merge history with modernity is what makes it truly unique. Whether it's through the towering Lanterna lighthouse (a symbol of Genoa's maritime soul), the narrow alleys that open into sunlit piazzas, or the scent of freshly baked focaccia from neighborhood bakeries, Genoa continues to evolve without ever losing its identity.

In 2025 and beyond, as Genoa continues to upgrade its infrastructure (such as the expansion of its airport connections and public transport systems), the city is positioning itself as a modern, sustainable destination with deep historical roots. Travelers who visit will not only witness the legacy of a once-powerful maritime republic, they'll also see a city confidently stepping into the future.

Genoa's Role in Italian History, Trade, and European Culture

While often overshadowed by cities like Rome, Venice, or Florence in popular imagination, Genoa holds a deeply rooted and highly influential role in Italian and European history. Its evolution from a medieval maritime republic to a modern cultural center is both complex and fascinating, and understanding its place in the broader context of European civilization reveals why Genoa is far more than a picturesque coastal stop.

A-Pillar of the Maritime Republics

Genoa's rise to power began in the Middle Ages, when it emerged as one of the four major Maritime Republics of Italy, alongside Venice, Pisa, and Amalfi. Between the 11th and 15th centuries, Genoa developed into a naval and commercial powerhouse. Its location—at the heart of Mediterranean trade routes—was ideal for maritime expansion. Genoese merchants and sailors traveled as far as the Black Sea, North Africa, and the Levant.

Genoa's fleet wasn't just massive—it was strategic. The city developed a reputation for shrewd diplomacy and pragmatic alliances. Genoa participated in the Crusades, not only for religious motivation but also as a means to secure lucrative trade concessions in conquered territories. It was during these times that the Genoese built trading colonies in places like Constantinople (modern-day Istanbul), Acre, and Cyprus, further extending their commercial reach.

At its height, Genoa controlled a significant part of the Western Mediterranean and even parts of the Eastern Mediterranean through a complex web of trade posts and alliances. Its rivalry with Venice was intense and defined much of the political and economic dynamics of the region. While Venice often took center stage in the Adriatic and Eastern Mediterranean, Genoa was dominant in the Western sphere.

The Genoese Financial Revolution

Perhaps less visibly glamorous than fleets and fortresses, but no less revolutionary, was Genoa's immense contribution to the development of modern finance. By the 13th and 14th centuries, Genoa had developed one of the earliest banking systems in Europe. Genoese bankers were among the first to use bills of exchange and sophisticated credit mechanisms that would eventually shape the foundations of international banking.

One of the most remarkable institutions was the Bank of Saint George (Banco di San Giorgio), founded in 1407. It is widely regarded as one of the oldest chartered banks in Europe. Far from being a simple depository, it managed public debt, collected taxes, and even governed some of Genoa's overseas colonies like Corsica. At various points, the bank wielded more influence than the Genoese government itself.

Genoa's financiers played a vital role in broader European affairs as well. During the 16th century, the Genoese banking elite became the financiers of the Spanish Empire, helping fund Charles V and later Philip II. These arrangements allowed Genoa to enjoy a financial renaissance even as its political and naval power waned.

Genoa in the Unification of Italy

Genoa's influence persisted into the modern era, including its role in the Risorgimento, the 19th-century movement that culminated in the unification of Italy. Genoa was the birthplace of Giuseppe Mazzini, one of the most important ideological leaders of Italian nationalism. His vision of a unified, republican Italy inspired thousands and laid the ideological groundwork for future unification efforts.

Mazzini's radical ideas found fertile ground in Genoa, a city with a long history of independence and self-governance. Genoa also served as a staging point for Giuseppe Garibaldi's Expedition of the Thousand in 1860. The city's ports and sympathies allowed Garibaldi to set sail for Sicily, beginning one of the most dramatic campaigns in Italian history. Genoa was officially incorporated into the Kingdom of Sardinia in 1815, which later formed the nucleus of unified Italy in 1861.

Trade, Industry, and Port Development

Genoa's strategic maritime position has never lost its relevance. Even in the 20th and 21st centuries, Genoa has remained one of Italy's busiest and most important commercial ports. From heavy industry and shipbuilding to modern logistics and container shipping, the Port of Genoa is a key node in both national and international trade.

Beyond the transport of goods, Genoa has embraced cruise tourism and marine services, attracting millions of passengers annually. As part of the "Blue Economy", Genoa is investing in sustainable maritime practices, balancing its industrial roots with ecological consciousness—an echo of its historical ability to adapt and evolve.

Cultural Contributions to Europe

Genoa's cultural legacy is as impressive as its political and economic history. Architecturally, the city boasts a stunning array of Renaissance and Baroque palaces, many of which were constructed during the height of its maritime glory. The Palazzi dei Rolli, a collection of aristocratic residences once used to host state visitors, is now recognized as a UNESCO World Heritage Site. They provide tangible evidence of Genoa's role as a major cultural and political capital.

Musically, Genoa was the birthplace of Niccolò Paganini, the 19th-century violin virtuoso and composer whose influence on Western classical music was monumental. His techniques and compositions are studied by musicians around the globe to this day.

In art and literature, Genoa has produced and inspired a number of great minds. The city has long been a melting pot of ideas—where Eastern goods and philosophies mingled with Western creativity. Genoa's libraries and universities have played a critical role in preserving medieval and Renaissance manuscripts, serving as a bridge between the past and the present.

Genoa and the Age of Exploration

One cannot speak of Genoa's historical impact without mentioning Christopher Columbus, arguably the most famous Genoese in history. Born in Genoa in 1451, Columbus would go on to change the course of world history with his voyages to the Americas under the Spanish crown. While Columbus did not sail under the Genoese flag, his origins in Genoa underscore the city's deep connection to seafaring and exploration.

Genoa honors its native son with Christopher Columbus' House (a reconstructed building believed to be near his birthplace), and a monument in Piazza Acquaverde. His legacy continues to attract visitors and historical inquiry.

Today, Genoa's historical and cultural significance is evident in every alleyway (caruggi), every museum, and every coastal breeze. From the grandeur of the Palazzi dei Rolli to the lingering aroma of fresh basil used in authentic Genoese pesto, the city offers a multi-layered narrative that speaks of resilience, innovation, and global interconnectedness.

Its story is not just one of past glories but of enduring relevance. Genoa is a living museum of Mediterranean civilization—a place where visitors can trace the currents of history that shaped not just Italy, but the wider world.

CHAPTER 3: HOW TO GET THERE AND AROUND

Leveraging Different Travel Options

To truly unlock Genoa's potential as a travel hub, understanding and leveraging its diverse transportation options, flights, trains, ferries, and domestic access is key. This guide will delve into how to navigate Genoa's transport network to maximize your exploration of the city and its stunning surroundings.

Flights: Arriving in Genoa and Beyond

Genoa is served by the Cristoforo Colombo Airport (GOA), conveniently located approximately 10 kilometers from the city center. While it's a regional airport, it offers connections to various European cities and some domestic routes.

Getting to and from Genoa Airport:

- Taxi/Private Transfer: The quickest and most direct option. A taxi ride to the city center typically takes around 20 minutes and costs approximately €24-€35. Private transfer services can be booked in advance for a hassle-free experience.
- AMT Volabus: This dedicated shuttle bus service is a popular public transport choice. It offers direct connections to Genoa's main train stations (Piazza Principe and Brignole) and the city center, with a journey time of about 25-30 minutes. Tickets are around €6.
- Train + Bus: While the cheapest option at around €1.60 for the train, it's less convenient for direct city center access. You would take a local bus from the airport to Genova Sestri Ponente train station (a 5-minute ride) and then catch a train to Piazza Principe or Brignole. This option is more suitable if your onward journey is by train from Sestri Ponente.

Leveraging Flights for Broader Exploration:

For travelers looking to explore beyond the immediate Ligurian region, Genoa Airport provides a gateway to other Italian cities or even nearby European destinations. Consider internal flights if you're short on time and planning to visit places further afield like Rome or Naples, although trains often offer a more scenic and relaxed journey for these routes.

Trains

Italy's efficient rail network makes trains an excellent choice for both intercity and regional travel from Genoa. The city boasts two main train stations: Genova Piazza Principe and Genova Brignole.

Genova Piazza Principe: Located centrally, near the historic center and the old port, it's often the preferred arrival point for tourists. It's a major hub with numerous regional and high-speed connections.

Genova Brignole: Situated further east in the city, also with good public transport links, Brignole serves as another important station for regional and national routes. It's particularly convenient for accessing the eastern part of Genoa and its residential areas.

Both stations offer metro stops, bus connections, and taxi services, ensuring seamless onward travel within the city.

Key Train Routes and Travel Times from Genoa:

- Milan: A frequent and popular route. High-speed trains can reach Milan Central Station in as little as 1 hour 33 minutes from Piazza Principe or 1 hour 45 minutes from Brignole.
- Turin: Direct trains connect Genoa to Turin in approximately 1 hour 33 minutes to 2 hours 14 minutes, depending on the service.
- Florence: Trains to Florence generally take around 2 hours to 3 hours 30 minutes, often with a change in Milan or another major hub. Direct services can be found.

- Rome: A longer journey, typically taking around 5 hours to 5 hours 30 minutes by high-speed train.
- Cinque Terre: The train is by far the most convenient way to explore the famous Cinque Terre villages. Frequent regional trains connect Genoa (Piazza Principe or Brignole) to Monterosso (around 1 hour to 1.5 hours) and La Spezia Centrale (around 50 minutes to 1 hour). From La Spezia or Levanto, you can easily connect to the Cinque Terre Express for direct access to all five villages.
- French Riviera (Nice, Marseille): While there are no direct high-speed trains, regional services connect Genoa to Ventimiglia on the Italian-French border. From Ventimiglia, you can easily change to French regional trains to Nice (total travel time around 3 hours 15 minutes with one change) or further to Marseille (a longer journey involving multiple changes, often over 6-9 hours by train).

Tips for Train Travel in Italy:

1. Book in Advance: Especially for high-speed (Frecciarossa, Italo) and popular routes, booking tickets in advance can secure better prices and ensure seat availability.
2. Validate Tickets: For regional trains, physical tickets often need to be validated in the green and white machines on the platform before boarding to avoid fines. E-tickets usually do not require this.
3. Understand Ticket Types: Familiarize yourself with different train types (e.g., Frecciarossa for high-speed, Regionale for local services) as ticket rules and pricing vary.
4. Check Station Names: Be aware of the two main Genoa stations (Piazza Principe and Brignole) when booking to ensure you select the most convenient one for your plans.

Ferries

Genoa's identity is intrinsically linked to its port, making ferries an exciting and practical mode of transport, particularly for exploring the Ligurian coastline and beyond.

Domestic Ferry Connections:

- Portofino: While direct ferries from Genoa to Portofino might be limited or require changes, you can often take a train to Santa Margherita Ligure or Camogli and then connect to a local ferry service for the scenic final leg to Portofino. This offers stunning coastal views from the sea.
- Cinque Terre (Seasonal): During warmer months, ferry services often connect Genoa to some of the Cinque Terre villages, offering a unique perspective of the coastline. This can be a pleasant alternative or complement to train travel.
- Sardinia (Olbia, Porto Torres, Golfo Aranci): Genoa is a major gateway for ferries to Sardinia. These overnight journeys are a popular way to reach the island with your vehicle.
- Sicily (Palermo, Termini Imerese): Ferries to Sicily also depart from Genoa, offering a direct link to the island.

International Ferry Connections:

Genoa's port serves as a significant international hub, with regular ferry services to:

- Corsica (Bastia, Ajaccio): Ideal for exploring the French island.
- Spain (Barcelona): A convenient option for connecting to the Iberian Peninsula.
- Tunisia (Tunis): For those venturing into North Africa.
- Morocco (Tangier Med): Another route connecting Italy to North Africa.

Tips for Ferry Travel:

1. Book in Advance: Especially for popular routes and during peak season, ferry tickets can sell out quickly.
2. Check Schedules: Ferry schedules can be seasonal and subject to change, so always verify departure times.
3. Consider Overnight Ferries: For longer journeys, overnight ferries often offer cabins for a comfortable sleep, allowing you to wake up at your destination.

Genoa's strategic location and well-developed transportation infrastructure make it an ideal base for exploring the Italian Riviera and beyond. By intelligently leveraging flights for long-distance arrivals, trains for efficient intercity and regional travel (especially to the stunning Cinque Terre), and ferries for coastal excursions and island adventures, visitors can craft a truly immersive and seamless Italian experience. Within the city itself, a combination of walking, buses, the metro, and Genoa's unique funiculars and lifts provides excellent domestic access, allowing you to discover every hidden gem of this captivating Ligurian capital. Understanding these diverse options empowers travelers to move with ease, making the most of their time in and around Genoa.

Navigating Genoa

Genoa may appear complex at first glance, built into the Ligurian coastline and framed by hills and harbor, but its public transportation system is a surprisingly well-integrated web of convenient options. Thanks to recent city-wide upgrades and tourist-friendly digital tools, navigating Genoa is not only easy but often scenic and enjoyable. From underground metro tunnels to hill-climbing funiculars, and from old-world alleys to a revitalized waterfront, getting around Genoa is an essential part of the experience.

Metro

Genoa's Metro system may be small in size, only one line, but it's incredibly efficient for connecting key parts of the city. The Genova Metro (Metropolitana di Genova) stretches across 7.1 kilometers with eight stations, running from Brin in the west to Brignole station in the east.

Stops include:

- Dinegro (near the ferry/cruise terminal)
- Principe (adjacent to the main train station)
- San Giorgio (perfect for tourists visiting the Aquarium, Porto Antico, and Palazzo di San Giorgio)
- De Ferrari (central to Piazza De Ferrari, museums, and major shopping streets)
- Brignole (connected to Genoa's second main train station and Via XX Settembre)

The trains are clean, modern, and frequent, typically running every 7–10 minutes from 6:30 AM to 9 PM, with extended hours during festivals and holidays. Tickets are inexpensive and part of the AMT public transport system, meaning one ticket works across the metro, buses, funiculars, and elevators. It's an ideal option for tourists moving between the harbor, city center, and key accommodation zones.

Funiculars

What makes Genoa uniquely appealing is how its topography merges with transportation. The city climbs into hills and ridges, and instead of cars or long staircases, Genoa offers a series of historic funiculars and public elevators—an engineering feat that's now a cultural experience.

There are four main funiculars:

1. Sant'Anna Funicular – Dating back to 1891, this funicular connects Piazza Portello to Corso Magenta and offers a ride into the charming residential and garden areas of the upper city.
2. Zecca–Righi Funicular – This one's especially scenic. Starting near Via Cairoli, it rises to Righi, which is the gateway to Forte Sperone and panoramic hiking trails.
3. Quezzi Funicular – A shorter but useful line, recently modernized, connecting lower neighborhoods with mid-hill residential districts.
4. Montegalletto Elevator-Funicular Combo – A true novelty. It's the only system in the world combining horizontal movement with vertical lift, linking Via Balbi to the Castello d'Albertis area. Tourists love it for the quirky engineering and the museum access it provides.

All funiculars are part of the AMT system, and free during promotional periods (as of 2024–2025) under the city's tourism mobility scheme. These rides are not just functional—they're immersive. As the cars ascend, the city unfolds beneath you in layers of red rooftops, narrow alleys, and glimpses of the sea.

Buses

Genoa's bus system is vast, and reliable, and covers the full spectrum of city neighborhoods, hillsides, ports, and suburbs. Buses are operated by AMT (Azienda Mobilità e Trasporti) and run from the early morning until late at night, with some lines offering night services.

Tourist-relevant routes include:

- Line 13 – Serves Castelletto and Corso Firenze, great for accessing scenic viewpoints.
- Line 17 – Runs through the city center and offers access to museums and shopping streets.
- Line 35 – Links the airport to the Sestri Ponente district.
- Airport Shuttle (Volabus) – Fast, air-conditioned, and direct, connecting Cristoforo Colombo Airport to both Principe and Brignole train stations. It's perfect for arriving or departing travelers.

Buses can be busy during rush hour, but they are well-maintained and provide digital timetables via the AMT Genova app, which helps users plan trips, buy tickets, and receive real-time traffic updates. The cost of a single ticket is modest and includes 90 minutes of unlimited travel, covering transfers between buses, metro, and funiculars.

Walking: Discovering Genoa on Foot

Despite its urban density, Genoa is one of Italy's most walkable cities—particularly for those looking to explore the old town. Much of the historic center, known for its "caruggi" (narrow medieval alleyways), is pedestrian-only and offers a true sense of Genoese life: laundry strung between buildings, ancient doorways, artisan shops, and the scent of focaccia around every corner.

Key walking zones include:

- Strada Nuova (Via Garibaldi) – A UNESCO World Heritage Site lined with opulent palaces and museums.
- Piazza De Ferrari – The beating heart of the city and a natural meeting point.
- Porto Antico – A wide-open pedestrian area ideal for relaxed waterfront strolls, especially at sunset.

While the hilly terrain might sound daunting, the presence of escalators, public elevators, and scenic staircases allows most tourists to move between elevations with ease. Comfortable shoes are essential, as cobblestones are common, and some streets are steep. Still, this walkability adds to Genoa's intimate charm.

Port Transport

Genoa is one of the Mediterranean's largest ports, and for travelers, that means a variety of water-based transport options—from international ferries to scenic boat rides.

Key services include:

- Traghetti (Ferries) – Genoa's port serves as a departure hub for ferries heading to Sardinia, Sicily, Corsica, Barcelona, and Tunis. Companies like Grandi Navi Veloci (GNV) and Moby Lines offer regular schedules from Terminal Traghetti, located near Dinegro Metro Station.

- Cruise Terminal (Stazione Marittima) – Welcomes international cruise ships. Tourists arriving by cruise can easily connect to the city via metro, shuttle buses, or even on foot to reach the historic center.
- Water Taxi & Port Boats – A developing service in Genoa's Porto Antico area, small boats and water taxis are sometimes available for scenic rides or to reach waterfront attractions like Bigo Elevator, Aquarium of Genoa, or Eataly.

Additionally, Genoa is investing in electrified port mobility and smart piers, making port transport cleaner and better integrated into the city's sustainable transport model. This is in line with the city's bid for "European Capital of Smart Tourism 2025."

What makes Genoa's transport landscape so compelling is not just its variety, but how deeply it connects to the city's soul. A funicular becomes a heritage ride; a metro stop brings you directly to a medieval gate; a port terminal doubles as an entry into centuries of maritime tradition. Whether you glide up the hillside in a glass elevator or weave through alleyways on foot, transportation in Genoa is more than just movement, it's part of the discovery.

With modern tools like the AMT Genova app, free public transit offers, and multilingual signage across the system, tourists in 2025–2026 will find that exploring Genoa is not only seamless but often unforgettable.

Ideal Periods to Travel to Genoa (Best Seasons & Events in 2025–2026)

Genoa, with its rich history, stunning architecture, and vibrant port, offers something for every traveler. The ideal time to visit largely depends on your preferences for weather, crowds, and events.

Best Seasons to Travel to Genoa

1. Spring (April - May) & Early Autumn (September - October): The Shoulder Seasons

Pros: This is widely considered the best time to visit. The weather is pleasant and mild, perfect for exploring the city's labyrinthine alleys (carrugi) and historical sites without the intense summer heat. Crowds are also considerably smaller than in peak summer, leading to more comfortable sightseeing and potentially lower prices for accommodation and flights. You might even enjoy an afternoon on the beach in late spring or early autumn.

Weather:
- April: Highs around 18°C (64°F), lows around 11°C (53°F).
- May: Highs around 22°C (71°F), lows around 16°C (60°F).
- September: Highs around 25°C (77°F), lows around 19°C (66°F).
- October: Highs around 21°C (69°F), lows around 15°C (59°F). October is the wettest month, so be prepared for some rain.

2. Summer (June - August): Peak Season

Pros: Long days and hot weather are ideal for beach activities and enjoying the Ligurian coast. The sea temperature is also warmest during these months, peaking in August at around 24°C (75°F), making it excellent for swimming. There's a lively atmosphere with many outdoor events.

Cons: Can be very hot, with temperatures often reaching 28°C (82°F) and occasionally higher. This is the busiest time for tourism, meaning larger crowds at attractions, higher prices for hotels, and potential difficulty with accommodation. Many Italians also take their holidays in August, particularly around Ferragosto (August 15th), which can lead to some local businesses being closed.

Weather:
- June: Highs around 25°C (77°F), lows around 19°C (67°F).
- July: Highs around 28°C (82°F), lows around 22°C (71°F).
- August: Highs around 28°C (83°F), lows around 22°C (72°F).

3. Winter (November - March): Low Season

Pros: Fewest tourists, leading to lower prices and a more authentic local experience. Great for exploring museums, art galleries, and churches.

Cons: Colder temperatures and higher chances of rain, especially in November, which is one of the wettest months. Some outdoor activities might be limited, and the days are shorter.

Weather:
- November: Highs around 16°C (61°F), lows around 11°C (51°F). This is the wettest month.
- December: Highs around 13°C (56°F), lows around 7°C (45°F).
- January: Highs around 12°C (54°F), lows around 6°C (43°F).
- February: Highs around 13°C (55°F), lows around 7°C (45°F).
- March: Highs around 15°C (59°F), lows around 9°C (48°F).

Notable Events in Genoa (2025–2026)

Keep in mind that event dates can sometimes shift, so it's always best to check official local tourism websites closer to your travel dates for the most up-to-date information.

Major Annual Events to Look Out For:

1. Salone Nautico (Genoa International Boat Show): Usually held in September. This is one of the largest boat shows in the world and a significant event for Genoa. In 2025, it's scheduled from September 18-23, 2025.
2. La Notte di San Giovanni (St. John's Night): Celebrations for Genoa's patron saint, St. John the Baptist, typically take place around June 24th. Expect music, street animations, and traditional festivities. In 2025, this is scheduled for June 23-24, 2025.
3. Suq Festival - Teatro del Dialogo: Often in June, this festival combines food, markets, music, and performances, focusing on intercultural dialogue. For 2025, it's listed as June 12-22, 2025.
4. Porto Antico EstateSpettacolo: A summer program of music and entertainment at the Old Port. This typically runs through the summer months. In 2025, it is listed as June 12 - August 31, 2025.
5. Nervi International Ballet Festival: A prestigious ballet festival usually held in the summer. In 2025, it is listed as June 28 - July 27, 2025.
6. Fiera di Natale (Christmas Market): If you're visiting in winter, the Christmas market provides a festive atmosphere, usually from December 1st to 24th in 2025.
7. Red Bull Cerro Abajo: This thrilling urban downhill mountain bike race typically takes place in August. For 2025, it's listed for August 24, 2025.

Other Ongoing Exhibitions and Cultural Events (2025):

Genoa often hosts numerous art exhibitions and cultural events throughout the year at venues like Palazzo Ducale and various museums. *In 2025, you can expect:*

1. World Press Photo Exhibition: Typically runs in late spring/early summer. In 2025, it's listed as April 30 - June 24, 2025.
2. "Genoa and the 19th Century" themed events: Several exhibitions, tours, and conferences celebrating Genoa's 19th-century history are scheduled throughout 2025 and into 2026.
3. Various cultural events and guided tours: Many museums and cultural institutions offer ongoing programs. Check the Visitgenoa website for specific details closer to your visit.

For 2026:

Beyond the regular public holidays (New Year's Day, Epiphany, Easter, Liberation Day, Labour Day, Republic Day, Ferragosto, All Saints' Day, Immaculate Conception, and Christmas), specific major events for 2026 are still being finalized. However, you can anticipate the annual recurring festivals and exhibitions to fall around similar times as 2025.

EFMI MIE 2026: An international conference on medical informatics, scheduled for May 25-28, 2026.

General Tip: For the most up-to-date and comprehensive event listings, consult the official Genoa tourism website (Visitgenoa.it) or local event calendars as your travel dates approach.

CHAPTER 4: TRAVEL RESOURCES AND PRACTICAL TIPS

Safety and Health Considerations for Tourists

When planning an unforgettable trip to Genoa, Italy, your health and safety should remain a top priority. This bustling port city is one of Italy's hidden gems, filled with winding alleys, grand palaces, and vibrant waterfronts. While Genoa is generally safe for tourists and known for its hospitality, staying informed about potential risks, healthcare facilities, emergency contacts, and local customs will help you make the most of your journey with peace of mind.

1. General Safety in Genoa

Genoa is considered a safe destination by European travel standards, with relatively low violent crime rates. Like most major cities, however, it is not immune to petty crimes such as pickpocketing, particularly in busy areas. Tourists should remain alert in crowded spots such as Piazza de Ferrari, Porto Antico, and the public transport system, especially around the train stations like Genova Piazza Principe and Genova Brignole.

Tips to Stay Safe:

1. Keep your valuables secure: Use a crossbody bag with a zipper and avoid keeping wallets or phones in your back pockets.
2. Avoid isolated alleys at night: The historic center, with its charming "caruggi" (narrow alleys), is beautiful during the day but can feel deserted after dark. Stick to well-lit areas and walk confidently.
3. Use authorized taxis or rideshares: If you're out late, use a registered taxi or rideshare app (like FreeNow or Uber) instead of hailing cars off the street.
4. Stay alert in public places: Markets like Mercato Orientale, though wonderful to explore, can attract pickpockets—especially during peak hours.

Local authorities are friendly and used to help tourists. If you ever feel uncomfortable or in danger, do not hesitate to contact the local police (Carabinieri or Polizia di Stato).

2. Emergency Contacts and Important Numbers

Familiarizing yourself with Italy's emergency numbers will give you an added layer of reassurance.

- General Emergency (EU-wide): 112
  This universal number connects you to police, ambulance, or fire services.
- Police (Carabinieri): 112
- Medical Emergencies: 118
- Fire Department: 115
- Coast Guard: 1530
- Tourist Helpline (Italian Government): +39 039 039 039

Tip: Many locals speak basic English, especially in service industries, but it can be helpful to carry a translation app or basic Italian phrases if you need to communicate in emergencies.

3. Health Facilities and Pharmacies

Italy's healthcare system is among the best in Europe, and Genoa has several excellent public and private hospitals, as well as English-speaking doctors and travel clinics.

Key Hospitals in Genoa:

Ospedale San Martino (San Martino Hospital)
- Address: Largo Rosanna Benzi, 10, 16132 Genova
- One of the largest hospitals in Italy, equipped with emergency and specialist services.

Galliera Hospital (Ospedale Galliera)

- Address: Mura delle Cappuccine, 14, 16128 Genova
- Centrally located and known for its efficiency and English-speaking staff.

Istituto Giannina Gaslini

- World-renowned for pediatric care. While geared toward children, it's also a reference for family emergencies involving minors.

Pharmacies (Farmacie):

Pharmacies are widespread across Genoa, often marked by a green cross. Most are open Monday to Saturday from 8:30 a.m. to 12:30 p.m. and 3:30 p.m. to 7:30 p.m. However, 24-hour pharmacies and rotating night shifts ensure medication access at all times. You can find after-hours pharmacies listed online or posted on the doors of regular pharmacies.

Tip: Bring a supply of essential medications and carry a translated medical prescription if you need to buy anything specific while abroad.

4. Health Insurance and Medical Coverage

Travelers to Genoa (and Italy in general) are strongly advised to carry valid travel insurance that covers:

- Emergency medical care
- Hospitalization
- Prescriptions
- Repatriation (in rare cases)

EU travelers with an EHIC (European Health Insurance Card) or EHIC replacement are entitled to emergency public healthcare during their stay. Non-EU visitors—such as those from the U.S., Canada, Australia, or the UK—should purchase travel insurance before departure. Some private hospitals may require upfront payment, so it's a good idea to have a copy of your policy documents and an emergency contact number for your insurer at hand.

5. Water, Food Safety, and Hygiene

The overall hygiene standards in Genoa are high. Tap water is safe to drink, and food served in restaurants or street markets generally meets health regulations.

Tips for Staying Healthy:

1. Hydration: Especially in warmer months, use refillable water bottles. Genoa has public drinking fountains across the city.
2. Seafood caution: Genoa is famous for its seafood. Make sure fish is well-cooked or properly stored—especially if you're trying raw dishes like acciughe marinate (marinated anchovies).
3. Street food hygiene: While sampling street food can be delightful, choose vendors with high turnover and clean practices.

Genoa is not a malaria-prone zone, and there are no required vaccinations for entry. However, being up-to-date on standard vaccines (MMR, Tetanus, Influenza, Hepatitis A) is always good practice.

6. COVID-19 and Post-Pandemic Travel Guidelines

As of 2025, Italy has moved past strict COVID-19 measures, and Genoa has resumed full tourist activity. However, it's smart to stay informed in case of unexpected surges or travel rule changes.

General Post-COVID Advice:

1. Carry a mask: While not mandatory, face masks may be recommended in healthcare settings or crowded indoor spaces like museums.
2. Digital health pass: Though not required in 2025, many venues still scan EU Green Passes or vaccine cards during high-traffic events.
3. Check airline requirements: Individual carriers may have differing policies about masking or testing.

For the latest updates, refer to Italy's Ministry of Health website or the Viaggiare Sicuri travel portal.

7. Sun, Sea, and Outdoor Safety

Genoa's coastal location and hilly terrain make it a paradise for outdoor lovers. Whether you're exploring Forte Diamante, sailing from the Porto Antico, or hiking in Parco delle Mura, it's important to take precautions.

Outdoor Safety Tips:

1. Sun protection: Wear sunscreen, sunglasses, and a hat—especially in summer. The Ligurian sun can be intense even in spring.
2. Stay hydrated: Dehydration can sneak up while walking the steep alleyways and historic fortresses.
3. Beach safety: Follow signage and lifeguard directions. Not all beaches have calm currents or sandy bottoms—some may be rocky.
4. Footwear: Wear comfortable, non-slip shoes. The cobbled alleys of Genoa's old town can be tricky to walk on.

8. Travel Scams and Tourist Awareness

While Genoa does not have the same reputation for scams as some larger cities, it's wise to remain cautious:

1. Avoid unofficial tour guides: Stick with accredited services or those recommended by the tourism board.
2. Beware of distraction techniques: A common petty theft method is to ask for directions or "accidentally" bump into you.
3. Count your change: In busy markets or taxis, always double-check your change and receipts.

When in doubt, visit the Tourist Information Centers around Porto Antico, Stazione Principe, or Via Garibaldi for safe travel resources and assistance.

Genoa is a safe, clean, and vibrant city that welcomes tourists warmly. Most visits are trouble-free, and with a few sensible precautions, travelers can relax and immerse themselves in the charm of Ligurian life. From emergency numbers and hospital access to knowing where to walk at night and how to stay hydrated while hiking, these safety and health considerations are designed to ensure your Genoa experience is as smooth and memorable as possible.

Bon viaggio, and stay safe as you explore this beautiful maritime gem on the Italian Riviera!

Essential Things to Pack for Your Genoa Adventure

Packing for a trip to Genoa means preparing for a rich blend of coastal charm, historical exploration, hilltop views, Mediterranean sunshine, and urban sophistication. Whether you're visiting for a short city break, a weeklong exploration of Ligurian culture, or a foodie adventure, packing smart will ensure a comfortable, safe, and memorable experience. In this section, we'll explore the essential things you should bring along for your Genoa adventure, categorized by clothing, travel gear, personal items, and practical extras.

1. Clothing Essentials

Genoa's coastal Mediterranean climate means mild winters, warm springs, and hot summers, with occasional sea breezes. Your clothing choices should reflect the season and the city's blend of outdoor walking and cultural venues.

Lightweight Layers

Even in summer, a light jacket or cardigan is recommended, especially for evenings or coastal breezes. During spring or autumn, pack long-sleeve shirts, hoodies, or sweaters for added warmth.

Comfortable Walking Shoes

Genoa's historical center is filled with narrow cobblestone alleys (caruggi) and steep streets, especially in older quarters like Castelletto or Righi. Pack well-cushioned walking shoes or sneakers that provide support for long sightseeing days. Avoid heels or thin-soled shoes.

Casual but Smart Attire

Most Italians dress smart-casual, even when just grabbing coffee. While tourists are welcome in all attire, consider packing stylish but relaxed outfits for daytime activities and a slightly dressier outfit for dinners, theaters (like Teatro Carlo Felice), or nightlife.

Summer Essentials

If visiting between May and September, you'll want:

- Breathable T-shirts and tank tops
- Lightweight shorts, skirts, or linen pants
- Sunglasses and a wide-brim hat
- Swimwear for beach visits or hotel pools

Modest Clothing for Religious Sites

Some churches or cathedrals may expect visitors to have covered shoulders and knees. Keep a scarf or wrap in your bag just in case.

2. Travel Documents and Copies

Your journey to Genoa will require valid and accessible travel documentation. Ensure you pack the following and keep digital backups saved securely (e.g., on your phone or email):

- Passport (valid at least 6 months beyond your return date)
- Visa or travel authorization, if required based on your nationality
- Flight or train tickets and confirmations
- Hotel reservations or accommodation contacts
- Travel insurance documents
- Copy of your ID card, in case of emergencies
- Emergency contact list and embassy information

A document organizer or travel wallet can help you keep these items tidy and accessible, especially at transport checkpoints.

3. Health and Safety Essentials

Being prepared for basic health needs will ensure that minor ailments or discomforts don't disrupt your exploration of Genoa's museums, piazzas, or waterfront.

Basic First-Aid Kit

Include small quantities of:

- Adhesive bandages for blisters
- Pain relievers (ibuprofen, paracetamol)
- Motion sickness tablets (especially if you plan to take boats or ferries)
- Antihistamines (for seasonal allergies)
- Hand sanitizer or sanitizing wipes
- Any prescription medications (with original packaging and a copy of your prescription)

Refillable Water Bottle

Genoa has clean public water fountains—refilling your eco-friendly bottle saves money and reduces plastic waste.

Sunscreen and Lip Balm

Especially important from spring through early autumn, SPF products will protect your skin while walking around sun-exposed coastal promenades or hillsides.

4. Tech and Digital Must-Haves

Your devices can help with navigation, translation, travel planning, and photography. Make sure you pack:

- Smartphone with charger and travel adapter (Italy uses type C, F, or L plugs)
- Portable power bank, for days when you're out exploring from morning to night

- Headphones or earbuds for train rides, museum audio guides, or walking tours
- Unlocked phone or eSIM for affordable data with a local or international SIM plan
- Travel camera, if you want high-quality photos beyond your phone

Download useful apps in advance, like:

- AMT Genova (for public transport info)
- Visit Genoa (for sightseeing ideas and virtual tours)
- Google Translate and Google Maps (offline mode)
- TripIt or similar for organizing your itinerary

5. Day Bag and Essentials for Daily Exploration

Each day in Genoa will likely involve a mix of walking, sightseeing, eating out, and perhaps a museum or boat ride. A lightweight backpack or crossbody bag is ideal. Inside, carry:

- City map or itinerary
- Guidebook or attraction list
- Sunscreen and hat
- Reusable shopping bag (handy for local markets)
- Notebook or travel journal
- Snacks like energy bars or fruit

If you're planning to visit popular attractions like the Aquarium of Genoa, Palazzo Reale, or the Lanterna, you may need timed entry tickets, which should be printed or saved digitally.

6. Optional but Useful Extras

Depending on your preferences and activities, here are a few extras that can enhance your Genoa adventure:

Travel Umbrella or Raincoat

Though Genoa is generally sunny, autumn and spring can bring sudden showers.

Lightweight Binoculars

Great for harbor views, hiking to Genoa's forts, or birdwatching at the Biosfera.

Swimsuit and Water Shoes

Perfect for day trips to beaches in Boccadasse, Nervi, or the Ligurian Riviera. Many rocky beaches benefit from water shoes.

Laundry Kit or Travel Detergent

For longer trips, especially if staying in apartments or hostels, this can help cut down on packing space.

Phrasebook or Italian Cheat Sheet

While English is understood in tourist areas, a small phrasebook or printed translation sheet can be a wonderful tool for respectful local interaction—especially in markets, bakeries, or less touristy neighborhoods.

7. Leave Space for Souvenirs

Genoa is known for artisanal items like:

- Pesto in jars
- Local olive oil and wine
- Ceramic and coral jewelry
- Handmade paper goods

Be sure to leave extra space in your suitcase or bring a foldable bag for take-home treasures.

Genoa is a destination that rewards prepared travelers—those who are equipped to explore winding alleyways, coastal landmarks, and cultural wonders. Packing with intention helps you stay comfortable, adaptable, and ready to dive into everything from a historic palazzo to a vibrant street food corner.

With the right essentials in your bag, your Genoa adventure will be more relaxed, immersive, and unforgettable.

Tourism Information: Navigating Genoa with Ease

To make the most of your visit, having access to accurate and up-to-date tourism information is key. Genoa offers several ways to get insights into its attractions, events, and services.

Official Tourist Information Centers (IAT Offices)

These offices are invaluable for maps, brochures, event listings, and expert advice from local staff.

- Ufficio IAT Garibaldi: Via Garibaldi, 12r, 16124 Genova. Phone: +39 0105572903. Email: info@visitgenoa.it. This is a central and easily accessible office.
- Ufficio IAT Aeroporto Cristoforo Colombo: Via Pionieri e Aviatori d'Italia, Aeroporto Piano Arrivi, 16154 Genova. Phone: +39 0105572903. Email: info@visitgenoa.it. Convenient for arrivals.
- Ufficio IAT Porto Antico: Ponte Spinola, 16126 Genova. Phone: +39 0105572903. Email: info@visitgenoa.it. Located at the vibrant Old Port area.

Online Resources:

VisitGenoa Official Website: www.visitgenoa.it/en: This is the official tourism portal for Genoa and an excellent resource for planning your trip. It provides information on attractions, events, accommodations, guided tours, and practical advice. You can also find contact details for their various offices.

Genoa City Tour: (https://www.genoacitytour.com/contacts): If you're considering a hop-on hop-off bus tour to see the city's highlights, this website offers contact information and details about their services.

Useful Apps for Your Genoa Adventure

In the digital age, a few well-chosen apps can be as indispensable as your passport. From navigation to public transport and even language translation, these apps will help you navigate Genoa like a local.

Navigation and Public Transport:

- Google Maps: Essential for getting around. It offers reliable public transportation routes (bus, metro, funiculars), walking directions, and real-time traffic updates. You can download offline maps to save data.

- AMT Genova: This is the official app for Genoa's public transport company (Azienda Mobilità e Trasporti). It's a must-have for commuters and tourists alike. *It features Real-time bus transits, route calculation, ticket purchase via credit card, Google Pay, or SMS, search for lines and stops, favorite stops, news and service updates, and information on various transport modes like metro, funiculars, lifts, and Navebus (boat service).*

  Note: While incredibly useful, some users have reported issues with international SIM cards. It's recommended for tourists to use it with a local SIM or stable Wi-Fi.

- Citymapper: A highly-rated public transportation app that provides comprehensive journey planning across various modes (bus, underground, ferries, walking). It can offer alternative routes and estimated travel times.

- BusDroid Genova: An unofficial Android application for public transport in Genoa, it allows users to check bus passage times at specific stops, find nearby stops, and save favorites. While unofficial, it uses data from AMT Genova's Infobus service and can be a good alternative if you encounter issues with the official app.

Language and Communication:

- Google Translate: Invaluable for bridging language barriers. It offers text translation, voice translation, and even instant camera translation for signs and menus. Crucially, it works offline, which is a significant advantage when data roaming charges are a concern.

- Duolingo: If you want to pick up some basic Italian phrases, Duolingo is a popular and engaging language-learning platform. Even a few key phrases can significantly enhance your interactions with locals.

- WhatsApp: Widely used in Italy, WhatsApp is the go-to app for free messaging and calls with friends and family back home, requiring only mobile data or Wi-Fi. It's also increasingly used by businesses and services for communication.

Exploring and Tourism:

- Play Phygital (Visitgenoa App): This official app from VisitGenoa offers an innovative way to explore the city. It features Virtual tours of Genoa (even from home!), creation of personalized itineraries, a 3D market to discover local shops and products, and "Genovini points" for engaging with the app, which can lead to prizes. It also uses augmented reality for on-site explanations.

- VoiceMap: Offers self-guided audio tours, including some for Genoa. These tours use GPS to automatically play audio as you walk, providing historical and cultural insights without needing to constantly look at your screen. Ideal for immersive exploration.

- Eventbrite / AllEvents: If you're interested in local events, concerts, exhibitions, or cultural gatherings, these platforms can help you discover what's happening in Genoa during your visit. While not Genoa-specific, they aggregate events from various sources.

Food and Convenience:

Uber Eats / Deliveroo: While Uber does not operate traditional ride-hailing services in Genoa, food delivery services like Uber Eats and Deliveroo are available. These apps allow you to order food from a wide range of local restaurants and have it delivered to your accommodation. Perfect for a cozy night in or when you want to try local cuisine from the comfort of your room.

Taxi Services:

- IT Taxi / Your Taxi App / Telepass Pay: Unlike many major cities, Uber's ride-hailing service is not available in Genoa. Instead, you'll rely on local taxi services. These apps allow you to book a taxi directly from your phone. You can also call a taxi by phone (+39 010 5966) or send a message via WhatsApp (+39 392 5966 123) to book a ride. Telepass Pay also allows you to pay for your ride through the app.

Money and Banking:

Wise (formerly TransferWise): If you're looking for an economical way to manage your funds in Italy and across Europe, a Wise Borderless account can be a practical option. It allows for multi-currency accounts and often offers favorable exchange rates.

By keeping these essential contacts and useful applications in mind, you'll be well-prepared to handle any situation that arises and fully immerse yourself in the beauty and culture of Genoa.

The Dos and Don'ts for Sustainable Tourism in Genoa

As one of Italy's most important historical port cities, Genoa blends medieval alleyways with modern waterfronts, rich culture with industrial legacy. In recent years, the city has made considerable efforts to foster sustainable tourism, earning praise as a finalist for the 2025 European Capital of Smart Tourism. As a visitor, your choices can directly contribute to preserving Genoa's charm, minimizing environmental impact, and supporting the local community. This section outlines the essential dos and don'ts for experiencing Genoa responsibly.

DO: Choose Sustainable Transportation Options

Do walk, cycle, or use public transport. Genoa's city center, including the famous caruggi (narrow alleyways), is best explored on foot. You'll not only reduce your carbon footprint but also uncover hidden piazzas, local bakeries, and artisan shops. The city also offers free public transport options (as of 2025), including funiculars, buses, and lifts through the AMT system. Apps like AMT Genova and Citymapper help you navigate without hassle.

Do use the metro or take the train for regional exploration. Genoa's modernized rail services make it easy to travel along the Ligurian coast to Cinque Terre, Portofino, and beyond. Using trains instead of rental cars minimizes congestion and emissions—especially vital in the narrow roadways around Genoa.

DON'T: Rely Heavily on Private Vehicles

Don't rent a car unless necessary. Genoa's old town is a ZTL (limited traffic zone) where cars are not permitted. Parking is limited and expensive, and navigating the historic city by car can be a nightmare. Instead, take the metro or local bus when needed, or use eco-friendly ride-sharing services that offer hybrid or electric vehicles.

DO: Stay in Eco-Friendly Accommodations

Do book certified green hotels or B\&Bs. Many of Genoa's hotels are committed to sustainability, offering energy-efficient lighting, waste reduction systems, and local sourcing for breakfast items. Look for accommodations with Green Key, EU Ecolabel, or EcoWorldHotel certifications.

Do consider locally owned guesthouses. These often use fewer resources and contribute directly to the local economy. Staying in a converted palazzo or family-run agriturismo on the city outskirts adds an authentic touch to your Genoese experience.

DON'T: Support Over-Touristed Chain Hotels

Don't prioritize international hotel chains over local options. Not only do many chain hotels use excessive energy and water, but they often divert profits away from Genoa's local economy. Consider instead a stay in Boccadasse, Castelletto, or Albaro for charming neighborhoods with character and fewer crowds.

DO: Support Local Artisans and Markets

Do buy from local producers and artisans. Genoa is famous for its handcrafted goods. ceramics, paper products, olive oils, and handmade pesto. Shopping at Mercato Orientale or the weekend artisan stalls near Porto Antico allows you to take home unique souvenirs while supporting small businesses.

Do eat locally and seasonally. Savor Ligurian specialties like focaccia al formaggio, pansoti con salsa di noci, and fresh seafood. When you dine at osterias or trattorias that are sourced from local farms and fishermen, you contribute to sustainable food practices.

DON'T: Buy Mass-Produced Souvenirs

Don't purchase cheap, imported trinkets. Mass-produced souvenirs contribute to waste and undermine the work of Genoa's local craftsmen. Avoid generic items stamped "Made in China" and instead seek handcrafted pieces that reflect Ligurian culture and artistry, like hand-bound journals, pesto kits, or Genoese ceramics.

DO: Respect Local Customs and Heritage Sites

Do learn a few Italian phrases. While many Genoese speak some English, learning basics like buongiorno (good morning), per favore (please), and grazie (thank you) is appreciated. It shows respect and effort toward cultural exchange.

Do follow guidelines at churches, museums, and historic sites. Many Genoese landmarks, such as San Lorenzo Cathedral or Palazzo Ducale, are sacred or culturally significant. Dress modestly when visiting religious sites, keep noise levels low, and don't touch artifacts unless allowed.

DON'T: Overcrowd Sensitive Areas or Be Disruptive

Don't overcrowd or rush through historical zones. Genoa's narrow alleyways weren't designed for large crowds, so be mindful of your impact—especially during festivals or summer months. Avoid following large tour groups that obstruct traffic flow and disturb daily life.

Don't act like a "tourist in a bubble." Sustainable tourism also means integrating respectfully with the community. Avoid playing loud music, littering, or treating Genoa like an amusement park. Instead, treat every street as if it were your neighborhood.

DO: Conserve Water and Energy

Do be conscious of your environmental footprint. Genoa, like many Italian cities, deals with seasonal water shortages. Limit long showers, reuse hotel towels when possible, and turn off lights, heating, or air conditioning when leaving your accommodation.

Do recycle. Use the color-coded bins around the city for separating paper, plastics, and organics. Genoa has been expanding its recycling programs and your effort helps sustain that progress.

DON'T: Leave a Trail of Waste

Don't litter or ignore disposal rules. Tossing wrappers or bottles in public places not only damages the environment but also disrespects local efforts to keep the city clean. If you're unsure where to dispose of something, carry it with you until you find a bin.

DO: Participate in Low-Impact Tours

Do choose small, guided tours or self-guided options. Walking tours of Genoa's historical center, food tours through caruggi, or hiking around Forte Diamante have minimal environmental impact. Companies that limit group sizes and educate travelers on Genoa's history and culture often adhere to sustainable practices.

Do consider volunteer tourism. Some organizations allow short-term tourists to join beach cleanups or cultural restoration projects. These opportunities let you give back to the city during your visit.

DON'T: Support Irresponsible Tourist Activities

Don't join over-commercialized or environmentally harmful tours. Avoid experiences that exploit animals, damage ecosystems, or overwhelm fragile neighborhoods. Also, be cautious of cruises that dock briefly and overload the city center—opt instead to stay a few nights and truly explore Genoa.

Sustainable tourism in Genoa means traveling with intention, respect, and awareness. Every choice, from where you sleep to how you move, what you eat, and how you behave, affects the city's future. By following these dos and avoiding the don'ts, you become more than a visitor; you become a conscious contributor to the preservation and celebration of Genoa's past, present, and future.

Language and Communication

When visiting Genoa, language and communication can deeply shape your travel experience. Though Italy is a major tourist destination, English is not always widely spoken, especially in non-touristy neighborhoods or when engaging with older locals. Understanding the linguistic environment in Genoa, along with some practical tips for communicating effectively, will make your trip smoother, more enjoyable, and far more enriching.

Primary Language: Italian

The official language spoken throughout Genoa and the Ligurian region is Italian. It is the language of everyday life, education, government, signage, public announcements, and media. While many tourist-facing establishments, such as hotels, museums, and some restaurants, do have staff who speak basic English, Italian remains the dominant means of communication.

In Genoa, Italian is spoken with a Ligurian accent, and in some areas, you may even hear Genoese (Zeneize), a traditional Ligurian dialect that is quite distinct from standard Italian. While Genoese is not commonly spoken in daily interactions anymore—especially among younger generations—it still appears in cultural expressions, literature, music, and signage in historical districts.

What About English?

English is understood to a basic or moderate degree in central areas of Genoa, especially:

- At hotels and hostels
- In museums and major attractions
- At the Porto Antico (Old Port), Aquarium, and ferry terminals
- In some upscale restaurants and cafes

However, don't expect fluency or complex conversations in English, particularly if you're venturing into residential districts, traditional osterias, or family-run stores. Genoa is not as heavily touristed as Rome or Florence, so English proficiency is lower compared to those cities.

That said, many younger locals, especially university students, have a working knowledge of English due to education reforms and exposure to online media. You might find it easier to communicate with the younger generation than with older Genoese citizens, who may only speak Italian or Genoese dialect.

Common Communication Scenarios & Tips

1. Restaurants and Menus

- In tourist-heavy areas, you may find bilingual menus in Italian and English.
- In traditional trattorias or local markets, menus may be exclusively in Italian.
- Don't hesitate to ask, "È disponibile un menu in inglese?" (Is an English menu available?)
- Use a translation app like Google Translate to scan menus and decipher ingredients.

2. Public Transport and Directions

- Metro stations and AMT transport maps often include some English, but announcements are primarily in Italian.
- If you're lost or need assistance, a simple question such as "Mi scusi, dov'è la stazione?" (Excuse me, where is the station?) can go a long way.
- Learn the names of places in Italian spelling, as locals may not understand English versions.

3. Shops and Markets

- Don't expect sellers to speak English at local markets like Mercato Orientale.
- Key phrases like "Quanto costa?" (How much is it?) and "Posso pagare con carta?" (Can I pay with a card?) are very useful.

- A friendly "Buongiorno" or "Buonasera" before asking questions creates a good impression.

Essential Italian Phrases for Travelers

Start your interactions politely:

Hello / Good day: Buongiorno (bwohn-JOOR-noh)
Good evening: Buonasera (bwoh-nah-SEH-rah)

When you need to be polite or grateful:

Please: Per favore (pehr fah-VOH-reh)
Thank you: Grazie (GRAHT-see-eh)
You're welcome: Prego (PREH-goh)

If you need to get someone's attention or apologize:

Excuse me / Sorry: Mi scusi (mee SKOO-zee) if addressing someone formally or Scusa (SKOO-sah) for informal situations.

For moments of confusion or when seeking assistance:

Do you speak English? Parla inglese? (PAR-lah een-GLEH-zeh?)
I don't understand: Non capisco (non kah-PEE-skoh)
Where is the bathroom? Dove si trova il bagno? (DOH-veh see TROH-vah eel BAN-yoh?)
How much does it cost? Quanto costa? (KWAHN-toh KOH-stah?)
I would like…: Vorrei… (voh-RRAY…) – very useful for ordering food or requesting items.
Check, please: Il conto, per favore (eel KON-toh, pehr fah-VOH-reh) – when you're ready to pay at a restaurant.

And in case of an emergency:

Help!: Aiuto! (ah-YOO-toh!)

Learning even a handful of these basic phrases will enhance your ability to interact politely and effectively during your trip.

Using Technology for Communication

1. Translation Apps

Apps like Google Translate, iTranslate, or Microsoft Translator can be invaluable, especially if they offer offline language packs. Use voice input or camera scanning to:

- Translate signs, menus, or product labels
- Communicate basic requests at hotels or shops
- Understand cultural or historical plaques

2. Messaging Apps

If you are staying with locals or booking tours via platforms like Airbnb or GetYourGuide, many hosts use WhatsApp to communicate. You can type messages in English and have them translated for smoother interactions.

3. Offline Phrasebooks

While digital tools are great, a small Italian phrasebook can be a reliable backup, especially in places with poor mobile reception.

Cultural Communication Tips

Italian communication goes beyond words, it includes tone, body language, and manners. Here are a few insights:

1. Gestures are common in Italian communication. Don't be surprised if locals use hand gestures to emphasize their points, they're part of the culture!
2. Italians often appreciate visitors making an effort to speak their language, even if it's just a few words.
3. Maintain eye contact when conversing, it's considered a sign of honesty and attention.
4. When entering shops or restaurants, always greet with "Buongiorno" or "Buonasera". Failing to do so may come off as rude.
5. Conversations may feel animated or expressive, this is perfectly normal and not necessarily a sign of conflict.

Regional Variations and the Genoese Dialect

You may occasionally hear snippets of Genoese (Zeneize), a Ligurian dialect with French and Arabic influences, particularly among older residents or in folk music and cultural events. While not necessary for tourists to learn, knowing this exists can add depth to your understanding of Genoa's rich maritime heritage.

Genoese differs quite a bit from Italian and is rarely written in official signage. However, some restaurant names, plaques, or street art may contain words like:

- Ma se ghe penso (If I think about it) – a line from a famous Genoese song
- Sciûsciâ e sciorbî (To blow and to sip) – referring to contradictory efforts or the impossibility of doing two things at once

These expressions are part of Genoa's identity and charm—and recognizing them adds flavor to your visit.

In Case of Miscommunication

If you're struggling to communicate, don't panic. Try the following:

- Speak slowly and clearly, but don't raise your voice.
- Write down what you want to say, visuals help a lot.
- Use gestures or point to items on a menu or map.
- Ask younger people for help, they are more likely to understand English.
- Keep conversations simple and avoid idiomatic English phrases.

Language barriers in Genoa are rarely insurmountable. With a bit of preparation, a few useful Italian phrases, and a positive attitude, you can navigate conversations with ease. Making an effort to communicate respectfully in the local language will not only open doors to smoother travel, it will often lead to warmer interactions, better service, and unforgettable connections with locals.

Whether you're ordering pesto trofie at a family-run trattoria, asking directions to the Lanterna, or chatting with a vendor at Piazza delle Erbe, remember: a smile and a "Grazie" go a long way.

CHAPTER 5: TOP 40 MUST-SEE

ATTRACTIONS AND ACTIVITIES IN GENOA

1. VILLA CROCE MUSEUM OF CONTEMPORARY ART

The Villa Croce Museum of Contemporary Art invites visitors into a cultural haven housed within a 19th-century neoclassical villa. Gifted to the city by the Croce family in 1951 and converted into a museum in 1985, it has become one of Genoa's main institutions for modern and contemporary visual arts. Set within a scenic public park with views of the sea, its surrounding landscape offers a tranquil retreat before even stepping inside the gallery.

Art enthusiasts will find a substantial collection of over 4,000 works, particularly strong in abstract and modern movements. Much of its strength comes from the Maria Cernuschi Ghiringhelli collection, which features Italian and international abstract pieces from the 1930s onward. The museum also showcases Genoese and Ligurian art from the mid-20th century and includes an important array of Italian graphic art. Notable artists represented include Lucio Fontana, Piero Manzoni, Dadamaino, and Giuseppe Uncini, as well as contemporary creators like Ben Vautier and Adrian Paci.

Beyond its permanent holdings, Villa Croce is known for its changing exhibitions, often devoted to emerging artists and contemporary themes. These exhibitions frequently go beyond visual arts, incorporating performance, literature, theater, and music to present cutting-edge cultural narratives. Each visit may offer something entirely different, reflecting ongoing global dialogues and encouraging visitor interaction with new artistic expressions.

The museum's historical setting adds dimension. The contrast between the classical interiors, retaining original 19th-century décor like fireplaces and painted ceilings, and the modern art installations creates a unique experience. A public-access library specializing in contemporary art further enriches the visit. Check the official website for current exhibits, opening times, and notes on any construction or accessibility updates, as renovations have been in progress to improve visitor services.

Though some parts of the building may be difficult to access for those with mobility issues, the villa's location in a lovely city park offers an enjoyable experience beyond the museum walls. With proximity to Genoa's historic center, it's a convenient cultural stop where art, architecture, and nature meet harmoniously.

2. CASTELLO D'ALBERTIS

Perched high on Montegalletto Hill, with sweeping views over Genoa and its bustling harbor, the Castello d'Albertis is a striking neo-Gothic mansion that now hosts the Museum of World Cultures. Constructed between 1886 and 1892 by the eccentric explorer Captain Enrico Alberto D'Albertis, the castle itself reflects his passion for global travel and eclectic tastes. Visitors are greeted with an unusual blend of Gothic Revival architecture and decorative influences from far-off cultures, making for a visually rich and atmospheric setting. Its lofty location provides panoramic vistas of Genoa and the surrounding Ligurian coastline, a bonus for those who make the trip.

The castle isn't just admired for its architecture, it serves as a curated archive of Enrico and his cousin Luigi Maria D'Albertis' expeditions to regions such as Africa, the Americas, Oceania, and New Guinea. The museum inside houses an intriguing collection of archaeological artifacts, ethnographic materials, seafaring instruments, vintage photographs, and model ships. Each room presents a different narrative, offering insight into the customs, histories, and material cultures of distant civilizations encountered by the D'Albertis family.

A centerpiece of the experience is the Museum of World Cultures, carefully arranged to highlight various cultural traditions from across the globe. This includes thematic sections like the Museum of Peoples' Music, where musical instruments from diverse regions are displayed. Some recent features have explored global medicinal practices, spotlighting healing traditions from Tibet, China, and India. Though the museum is generally tourist-friendly, limited English signage in some areas means visitors may benefit from a guide or translation app for a fuller understanding.

To reach this mountaintop destination, several options are available. Though a walk from Genoa Piazza Principe station is steep, many opt for the Ascensore Castello d'Albertis-Montegalletto, a hybrid lift and funicular that makes the journey both easier and more memorable. Once at the summit, allow time not just for the exhibits, but also to enjoy the peaceful gardens surrounding the castle, where benches and shaded spots invite quiet reflection amid spectacular views.

The Castello d'Albertis encourages visitors to consult its website for the latest updates on tickets, opening times, and temporary shows. Keep in mind that the museum may close during severe weather warnings classified as "RED." Overall, a visit here blends travel, history, and aesthetics into a fascinating encounter with the wider world, all without leaving Genoa.

3. PALAZZO REALE (ROYAL PALACE MUSEUM)

The Palazzo Reale, also known as the Royal Palace Museum, is a stunning showcase of Genoa's aristocratic legacy. Built in the 1600s for the affluent Balbi family, the property later came under the control of the Durazzo family before serving as a residence for the Savoy royal dynasty. Its opulent past is still visible today, with carefully preserved interiors highlighting the grandeur of noble life. The palace forms part of the UNESCO-listed "Strade Nuove and Palazzi dei Rolli," celebrated for its cultural and architectural importance to the city's urban development.

Step into a world of elegance and sophistication as you tour the palace's dazzling Baroque and Rococo interiors. The museum's collection features over a hundred artworks by prominent painters like Van Dyck, Tintoretto, Luca Giordano, Guercino, and Bassano, alongside distinguished Genoese artists. Beyond the paintings, the palace is a masterpiece in its own right, with lavishly frescoed ceilings, ornate stuccoes, and original period furnishings that recreate the splendor of Genoa's noble households.

The standard visit takes you through an impressive entrance hall decorated with 18th-century stuccoes, the stately courtyard of honor, and a tranquil hanging garden with picturesque views of Genoa and its harbor. The crown jewel is the noble apartment on the upper floor, featuring the Throne Room, a gilded Ballroom, and a glittering Hall of Mirrors that rival those of European royal courts. With gilded décor, delicate chandeliers, and sumptuous drapes, the experience is nothing short of regal.

Additional spaces such as the Apartment of the Hereditary Princes (or Duke of the Abruzzi's Apartment) are occasionally opened for special events, offering further insight into the palace's storied past. To fully enjoy the visit, plan to spend 2 to 3

hours. Checking the museum's official site ahead of time is recommended for current schedules and special exhibits, as opening hours can fluctuate.

The Palazzo Reale is easily reachable from Genoa Piazza Principe train station. While the experience is grand and immersive, lighting in some galleries may be subdued to protect artworks. Audio guides are available and provide enriching context for both the museum's art collections and its royal legacy.

4. GALATA MUSEO DEL MARE

The Galata Museo del Mare is the largest maritime museum in the Mediterranean and one of its most innovative. Housed in the historic Palazzo Galata, once a shipyard for Genoese galleys, the museum fuses old-world architecture with state-of-the-art exhibition techniques. Spanning five floors and 31 immersive galleries, it traces five centuries of maritime tradition and Genoa's powerful relationship with the sea.

The museum offers an exciting, interactive experience, unlike traditional displays. Among the highlights is a meticulously crafted full-size model of a 17th-century galley, where visitors can step aboard and imagine life at sea. Other ship reconstructions give the museum a dynamic atmosphere where guests can engage directly with history. Virtual sailing simulations and sailor lifestyle recreations add depth to the hands-on experience.

A deeply moving section titled "La Merica" focuses on the stories of Italian emigrants leaving Genoa for new lives overseas. Through interactive displays, including a recreated Atlantic crossing complete with engine sounds and ocean views, visitors can feel the emotional weight of those journeys. This exhibit offers profound insight into the hopes and hardships of migration during the 19th and 20th centuries.

For those seeking an even more immersive experience, the adjacent Nazario Sauro S-518 submarine can be toured while afloat. This Cold War-era naval vessel is Italy's first museum submarine in water, and although entry requires a separate ticket, it provides an intriguing look into the tight, functional world of submarine life. Claustrophobic visitors should take caution, as the space is extremely compact.

In total, a visit to Galata Museo del Mare can easily occupy 2 to 3 hours. From ancient charts to navigational instruments and

evocative marine art, the museum's scope is both wide and engaging. Most areas are accessible to wheelchair users, though the submarine is not. Rich in detail and experience, the museum invites guests to board a voyage through Genoa's enduring maritime identity.

5. GALLERIA NAZIONALE DI PALAZZO SPINOLA

The Galleria Nazionale di Palazzo Spinola opens a window into Genoese high society and its artistic heritage. Built in the 1500s by Francesco Grimaldi and later home to the Pallavicini, Doria, and Spinola families, the palazzo became public in 1958 through the generous donation of the Spinola heirs. It now preserves the memory of a city shaped by its seafaring wealth and noble traditions.

Visitors are treated to both a historical residence and an art museum. The lower two floors retain much of their original opulence, showcasing frescoed ceilings, marble flooring, antique furniture, and Asian-inspired décor. These rooms capture the luxurious ambiance of Genoa's golden age, allowing guests to experience the lifestyle of the city's powerful merchant elite firsthand.

The upper levels house the National Gallery of Liguria, a rich repository of fine art. The collection is especially strong in Italian and Flemish Renaissance works, with standout pieces by van Dyck, Rubens, Joos van Cleve, Giordano, and Strozzi. A highlight for many is Antonello da Messina's "Ecce Homo." The collection continues to grow with periodic additions, reflecting Liguria's evolving artistic legacy.

Take note of the intentional contrast between the historic décor below and the clean, curated exhibition layout upstairs. Due to renovation works in 2025, the third and fourth floors were temporarily closed for upgrades, with some works relocated, visitors are encouraged to confirm current conditions online before visiting.

Palazzo Spinola is a proud member of Genoa's Palazzi dei Rolli and part of its UNESCO designation. Allocate ample time to explore both historical and artistic dimensions.

The site is wheelchair accessible, making it an excellent stop for all types of travelers eager to experience Genoa's cultural and aesthetic depth.

6. MUSEO D'ARTE ORIENTALE EDOARDO CHIOSSONE

Set within the tranquil Villetta Di Negro park, the Museo d'Arte Orientale Edoardo Chiossone holds one of Europe's most important Asian art collections. Housed in a mid-century rationalist structure designed by Mario Labò, the museum honors Edoardo Chiossone, a Genoese engraver who spent over two decades in Japan collecting rare works. With more than 15,000 artifacts, the museum reflects a deep cultural connection between East and West.

The museum's displays are thoughtfully arranged by theme and technique, offering a multifaceted look at East Asian craftsmanship. Visitors will find stunning Buddhist statues, ornate Samurai armor, and a wide range of decorative arts, including ceramics, lacquerware, and bronzes. These pieces illuminate centuries of tradition and artistic refinement in Chinese and Japanese culture.

Due to preservation needs, delicate items like Ukiyo-e prints, rare books, and painted scrolls are not permanently on display. Instead, they rotate during temporary exhibits. Those with specific interests should consult the museum's website or contact staff in advance to confirm the availability of particular works.

Adding to the experience is the surrounding Villetta Di Negro park, ideal for a pre- or post-visit stroll. The serene gardens and city views enhance the museum outing with a peaceful natural atmosphere. Wearing comfortable footwear is advisable if you plan to explore the park's winding paths.

It is accessible to visitors with disabilities, though checking ahead is always wise.

7. MUSEO DI SANT'AGOSTINO

Housed in a restored 13th-century Augustinian monastery that survived wartime damage, Museo di Sant'Agostino stands as both an artifact and a collection space. Two striking cloisters, including a rare triangular one, offer a dramatic introduction to this historic complex.

Inside, the museum offers a chronological journey through Ligurian artistic development. Emphasis is placed on sculpture, though other media such as frescoes, ceramics, and woodworking are also on display. Exhibits highlight the cultural identity of Genoa through art, charting its evolution from a medieval port to a modern cultural center.

A must-see is Giovanni Pisano's funerary monument of Margherita di Brabante, a 14th-century masterpiece that commands reverence despite its fragmented state. Additional works by Cambiaso and Puget, alongside salvaged sculptures from destroyed churches, provide further insight into the city's artistic resilience and grandeur.

Temporary exhibitions and public programs are regularly held, adding fresh context to the museum's permanent displays. The adjoining church, Genoa's last remaining Gothic example, features a dramatic black-and-white façade and a decorative rose window. The view of the gardens and tiled bell tower offers a peaceful conclusion to the visit.

Easily accessed by metro via Sarzano/Sant'Agostino station, the museum is close to other historic attractions. Combination tickets are often available, families and young children can often enjoy free admission, making it an ideal stop for all ages.

8. MUSEO DI STORIA NATURALE

At Via Brigata Liguria 9, the Museo Civico di Storia Naturale Giacomo Doria holds the title of Genoa's oldest and most respected museum devoted to natural sciences. Established in 1867 by the renowned explorer and scientist Giacomo Doria, it moved into its current grand structure in 1912. The museum enjoys global acclaim for its immense scientific archives, containing millions of zoological, botanical, geological, and fossil specimens collected from all corners of the globe. It is a magnet for science lovers and families alike, offering a rich encounter with the wonders of nature.

Guests are invited to explore two expansive floors with 23 exhibition rooms filled with detailed displays. The ground floor features mammal species, including a fossilized Italian Elephant and an impressive collection of marsupials, along with a large African Savannah diorama. This level also contains a hall for temporary themed exhibitions and an amphitheater for events such as screenings and lectures, offering an interactive layer to the museum experience.

The first floor focuses on other vertebrates like birds, reptiles, amphibians, and fish. Meanwhile, invertebrate and insect diversity is explored in two specialized rooms. A standout is the "Cell Room," where a dramatically enlarged 3D cell model reveals microscopic inner workings in a way that's both accessible and awe-inspiring. The tour finishes with an extensive mineral collection, showing off the dazzling variety of Earth's geological structures.

While the museum is usually accessible via ramp and equipped with accessible restrooms, there have been recent disruptions. As of April 8, 2025, the museum is temporarily closed due to structural repairs and conservation efforts. Although public access to the exhibits is currently restricted, the museum continues to host learning programs and events. Visitors are advised to consult the official website for reopening schedules and to check on elevator availability, which was previously out of service.

Though temporarily closed, the Museo di Storia Naturale Giacomo Doria remains a cornerstone of Genoese scientific culture. Upon reopening, it will once again provide immersive experiences for nature lovers of all ages, delivering educational value and a deeper appreciation for Earth's living and non-living treasures.

9. MUSEO DEL RISORGIMENTO

Located within Giuseppe Mazzini's birthplace, the Museo del Risorgimento is a deeply meaningful destination dedicated to Italy's struggle for unification. This Genoese museum immerses visitors in the revolutionary ideas and historical events that shaped modern Italy. Organized into twelve thematic rooms, the exhibitions begin with Genoa's 1746 uprising against Austrian rule, featuring the legendary figure Balilla, and proceed through events such as the Jacobin Republic, Napoleonic annexation, and integration into the Kingdom of Sardinia.

A central attraction is the Giuseppe Mazzini exhibit, set in the actual apartment where he was born. It includes a preserved bedroom and memorabilia showcasing his early years. One of the most important displays features the original handwritten draft of Italy's national anthem, "Fratelli d'Italia," penned by Goffredo Mameli, another prominent Genoese patriot. These personal touches bring Italy's nation-building narrative to life.

Further galleries cover defining events such as the short-lived Roman Republic and Genoa's lesser-known rebellion in 1849. A considerable section is devoted to Garibaldi's "Expedition of the Thousand," complete with uniforms worn by the Red Shirts and items from the Carabinieri Genovesi. The timeline extends to World War I and the Resistance, with artwork, photos, official documents, weapons, and flags illustrating a century of conflict and change.

One standout feature is the museum's focus on Genoese contributions to national unity. While most labels are in Italian, visitors with some background knowledge of the Risorgimento will better appreciate the significance of the artifacts. Highlights include Mazzini's guitar from his London exile, a silk Flag of the Thousand from 1860, and the original copy of the Act of Surrender signed by German troops in Genoa on April 25, 1945.

This compact museum is best experienced at a relaxed pace. Though small in scale, its exhibitions are dense with meaning and patriotic symbolism. It's an essential stop for those interested in modern Italian history and Genoa's critical role in shaping the nation.

10. MUSEO DIOCESANO

The Museo Diocesano in Genoa offers a spiritual and artistic retreat nestled inside the former residence of the San Lorenzo Cathedral canons. Tucked behind the cathedral at Via Tommaso Reggio 20r, and entered through a beautiful 12th-century cloister, the museum provides a quiet and reflective space away from city life. The intimate layout invites visitors to explore centuries of religious art and ecclesiastical heritage in a peaceful setting.

Inside, the museum presents an array of treasures from Genoa's diocesan territory, including sculptures, illuminated manuscripts, liturgical textiles, and paintings. Among the most unique items are the "Passion Cloths", blue-dyed linen panels with white lead designs dating back to the 1500s. These rare textiles are not only valuable religious artifacts but also represent an early use of indigo dyeing techniques that eventually inspired denim, linking sacred traditions with modern fashion.

The building itself is layered with history, constructed between 1176 and 1184 atop ancient Roman foundations. Its architecture has evolved through centuries of renovations, becoming a monument in its own right. Particularly striking is the Romanesque-style cloister, complete with two tiers of arches and columns, while the first floor reveals fragments of medieval frescoes. The structure seamlessly integrates with the museum's narrative, creating a dialogue between sacred space and historical storytelling.

Beneath the main exhibits lies an archaeological section containing Roman-era artifacts and burial relics. This subterranean layer reveals an even older chapter in Genoa's story, offering visitors a rare opportunity to connect with its deep roots. While much of the museum is accessible by elevator, some portions, especially where the Passion Cloths are displayed, may involve stairs, so visitors with mobility concerns should plan accordingly.

In all, the Museo Diocesano offers a unique look into the religious and artistic identity of Genoa. It's a serene and intellectually rewarding stop for anyone interested in church history, medieval art, or Romanesque architecture. A visit of one to two hours is ideal, and checking the official website beforehand will help ensure you catch any special exhibitions or updated visitor information.

11. STRADA NUOVA (VIA GARIBALDI)

Strada Nuova, formally known as Via Garibaldi, is a spectacular legacy of Genoa's Renaissance grandeur. Designed in the 16th century as an ambitious urban project, this short yet majestic 250-meter stretch was intended to showcase the wealth and influence of the city's elite. Today, it forms the heart of the UNESCO-listed site "Le Strade Nuove and the Palazzi dei Rolli," noted for its architectural brilliance and urban vision. Closed to traffic, this elegant pedestrian promenade offers a step back into a world of aristocratic opulence, surrounded by perfectly preserved Renaissance and Baroque architecture.

As you walk the length of Via Garibaldi, you're flanked by a series of magnificent palaces, once homes to Genoa's ruling families and part of the "Rolli" system, whereby selected residences hosted visiting state dignitaries. These grand buildings feature elaborate façades, ornate entrances, stunning inner courtyards, and lush private gardens. While several still function as private homes or administrative buildings, many have been converted into public museums or art galleries, providing rare access to their sumptuous interiors.

For those keen on art and history, the Strada Nuova Museums, comprising Palazzo Rosso, Palazzo Bianco, and Palazzo Doria Tursi, are essential stops. Palazzo Rosso preserves the domestic elegance of a noble 17th-century residence, while Palazzo Bianco displays an excellent collection of European art, including pieces by Van Dyck and Caravaggio. Palazzo Doria Tursi, now home to the City Hall, offers a blend of decorative arts and historical memorabilia, including the prized violin "Il Cannone" once played by Paganini.

A visit to Via Garibaldi invites deep exploration, as the real treasures are often found behind the grand doors, lavishly frescoed ceilings, marble staircases, and secret gardens. Check museum schedules ahead of time, as hours and accessibility can differ. The biannual "Rolli Days" provide a rare opportunity to access palaces typically closed to the public, allowing for an even deeper immersion into Genoa's aristocratic legacy.

Via Garibaldi is easily reached on foot and serves as a cultural highlight of any city tour. Be sure to wear comfortable footwear, as there's plenty to discover in and around these timeless palaces. And don't forget to look skyward—the artistic grandeur often stretches far above street level.

12. SAN LORENZO CATHEDRAL

At the heart of Genoa's old city sits the awe-inspiring San Lorenzo Cathedral, or Cattedrale di San Lorenzo, one of the city's most iconic religious landmarks. This cathedral showcases a mesmerizing fusion of Gothic, Romanesque, and Baroque styles. Its most recognizable feature is its dramatic black-and-white striped marble façade, emblematic of Ligurian medieval design. Twin bell towers flank the structure—although one remains famously incomplete—offering a reminder of its long and storied construction history.

Inside, visitors encounter a rich mosaic of architectural evolution. The layout features a central nave with two flanking aisles, vaulted ceilings, and soaring arches, giving the space both grandeur and spiritual reverence. The cathedral is filled with artistic treasures—frescoes, marble sculptures, and elaborately decorated chapels. Of special significance is the Chapel of Saint John the Baptist, housing the relics of Genoa's patron saint, brought back during the First Crusade, which remains a focal point of religious devotion.

Tourists should prepare for a visit that is both culturally immersive and spiritually moving. Modest dress is expected—covering shoulders and knees—and photography is typically allowed without flash. Among the more curious relics is an unexploded World War II bomb resting in the right nave, a somber yet powerful reminder of the church's miraculous survival amid wartime destruction. This juxtaposition of sacred space and wartime memory adds depth to the overall visit.

The cathedral is also home to the Museo del Tesoro (Treasury Museum), accessible via the interior, where sacred artifacts are preserved. One of its most intriguing items is the Sacro Catino, a green glass vessel believed by some to be the Holy Grail. This museum complements the cathedral experience by offering context to the religious objects and revealing centuries of Genoese ecclesiastical heritage through jewels, manuscripts, and relics.

To truly appreciate the cathedral, visitors should allow time for both the main building and the museum. Those who climb the towers are rewarded with expansive views of Genoa's rooftops and the Ligurian Sea. Guided tours are often available, enriching the experience with historical anecdotes and architectural insights. Afterward, the lively Piazza San Lorenzo is perfect for lingering—whether browsing nearby artisan shops or enjoying a coffee amid the city's enduring beauty.

13. PALAZZO DUCALE

Palazzo Ducale, Genoa's former Doge's Palace, is one of the city's most majestic and historically significant buildings. Once the seat of the Genoese Republic and residence of the Doges, this monumental complex has evolved into Genoa's main cultural venue. Situated between Piazza Giacomo Matteotti and Piazza De Ferrari, the palace reveals its layered history through its dramatic facades and architectural elements. Originally built in the late 1200s, the building has undergone extensive reconstructions, particularly after a 1777 fire, resulting in a blend of Gothic, Mannerist, and Neoclassical features.

Today, Palazzo Ducale is a thriving hub for arts and public life. Its extensive halls host rotating exhibitions, music festivals, conferences, and civic events year-round. After a significant restoration project between 1980 and 1992, much of the palace's original grandeur was revived, allowing visitors to explore its vast and varied interior while experiencing contemporary cultural programming in a historic context. It is a place where the past and present interact seamlessly.

Inside, tourists can expect architectural highlights like the Salone del Maggior Consiglio and Salone del Minor Consiglio, both historically significant chambers adorned with frescoes and often used for large-scale events. Another notable site is the Torre Grimaldina (or Torre del Popolo), formerly used as a prison. Climbing this tower not only offers sweeping views of the city but also allows a glimpse at the graffiti and etchings left by its political prisoners—poignant remnants of the city's more turbulent eras.

Visitors are encouraged to observe the building's diverse stylistic layers. From medieval foundations to Neoclassical renovations, each room tells a part of Genoa's story. Though much of the palace is free to explore, some special exhibits or tower visits may require a separate ticket. Checking the Palazzo's official website in advance is advised to confirm what's open during your visit.

Palazzo Ducale is easily accessible whether you arrive by metro (De Ferrari station), on foot from the old town, or by local buses. It's a perfect launching point for further exploration, with shops, cafes, and other landmarks just steps away. Whether you're drawn by history or modern creativity, this palace is an essential stop for every Genoa itinerary.

14. CHRISTOPHER COLUMBUS' HOUSE

Genoa's Casa di Colombo, or Christopher Columbus House, pays tribute to the early life of the famous explorer. Located at Via di Porta Soprana, 16121 Genova, just beyond the medieval city walls, this two-story reconstruction stands as a symbolic link to the birthplace of the man who would cross the Atlantic and change world history. Though the original 15th-century home was destroyed during the 1684 French bombardment, the present building was rebuilt in the 18th century based on historical evidence and oral tradition.

Inside, visitors find a small yet evocative space. The lower level is thought to have served as the workshop of Columbus's father, Domenico, a wool weaver by trade. The upper floor was the family's living quarters, giving visitors a sense of the modest beginnings from which the famed navigator arose. Informational displays provide context about the Columbus family's life and Genoa's culture during the 1400s, helping visitors connect the simple structure to broader historical themes.

While the building itself is humble, its real value lies in its historical significance. The house is part of a larger medieval setting that includes the Porta Soprana gate and the reconstructed Cloister of Sant'Andrea. These adjacent attractions help round out the experience, offering additional layers of context and visual appeal. Together, they create a small yet compelling historical complex that captures the spirit of Genoa's past.

Due to the age and layout of the building, accessibility may be limited, especially for those with mobility issues. However, the house's location near other major landmarks makes it an easy addition to a walking tour. Opening hours vary, so it's wise to check in advance. Guided tours are available and highly recommended—they bring added depth to the site's historical narrative and offer insight into Columbus's formative years and Genoa's maritime legacy.

Though reconstructed, a visit to the Casa di Colombo offers a meaningful moment of reflection. It reminds visitors of the humble origins behind one of history's most influential figures and celebrates Genoa's role in the Age of Exploration. It's a brief but rewarding stop for those curious about where Columbus's extraordinary journey began.

15. ST ANDREW'S CLOISTER

The Cloister of St. Andrew (Chiostro di Sant'Andrea) offers a peaceful pocket of medieval history in modern Genoa. Originally part of a Benedictine monastery built in the 12th century, the cloister was relocated in 1905 after the original complex was demolished to make room for urban expansion. Today, it stands beside the Columbus House and Porta Soprana, beautifully preserved with slender Gothic columns and ornately carved capitals. This tranquil site provides a contemplative setting amidst the city's hustle, where stone craftsmanship speaks of centuries past.

Though modest in size, the cloister makes a lasting impression. Nestled within a quiet garden, it's a favorite spot for artists, students, and locals who come to sit, read, or sketch. The serenity it offers makes it feel worlds apart from the nearby bustling city streets. While the surrounding monastery is long gone, the cloister alone remains a powerful symbol of the city's dedication to conserving its historical legacy.

Historically, this cloister served the Portoria neighborhood's fishermen and sailors, offering a spiritual refuge. Its preservation and relocation represent an important civic effort to protect cultural heritage. By placing it alongside other iconic sites like the Columbus House, Genoa has woven the cloister into its broader historical narrative, reinforcing its value as more than just a decorative ruin.

Today, the space occasionally transforms into a small cultural venue, hosting temporary exhibitions and concerts. Its location in Genoa's historic district makes it a convenient stop for visitors exploring nearby medieval attractions. As part of a walking tour, the cloister offers a moment of rest, reflection, and deeper appreciation for the city's medieval roots.

St. Andrew's Cloister is generally open Tuesday to Sunday, with variable closing hours and closures on Mondays. Easily reached from Piazza De Ferrari or the De Ferrari metro station, it is a gentle detour worth taking. Allow 15 to 30 minutes to explore and soak in the details before moving on to the next site in Genoa's rich historic landscape.

16. LANTERNA DI GENOVA (THE LIGHTHOUSE OF GENOA)

The Lanterna di Genova, or Genoa Lighthouse, is an enduring symbol of the city's maritime legacy, continuing to guide ships with its steady beam. Standing 77 meters high atop a 40-meter rock foundation, the structure reaches an impressive total elevation of 117 meters above sea level, ranking as the tallest lighthouse in the Mediterranean and one of the tallest masonry lighthouses in the world. Originally constructed in 1128 and rebuilt in 1543, it still functions today, flashing its beacon every 20 seconds. As both a historical monument and an active part of the port's operations, it bridges the city's nautical past with its present.

A visit to the Lanterna goes beyond admiring its size, it includes a scenic approach via the "Lanterna promenade," an 800-meter pedestrian walkway partially tracing the 17th-century city walls. This walk provides sweeping views of Genoa's harbor and urban landscape. At the base of the lighthouse, a multimedia museum brings the maritime heritage to life through engaging video exhibits and archival displays. This modern museum helps contextualize the Lanterna's role in the growth and development of Genoa and its surrounding region.

Those who make the ascent can climb 172 steps to a terrace partway up the tower. From this vantage point, you'll enjoy striking views of the port, historic old town, and Ligurian coastline. Though the full height is not accessible, the observation deck offers an unmatched perspective of Genoa's maritime geography. The climb requires moderate physical effort, so visitors should be prepared, but the panoramic rewards make the effort worthwhile.

Before visiting, it's essential to verify current schedules since the Lanterna and museum are generally open only on weekends and public holidays, usually in the afternoons. Weather conditions may affect operations, and during busy times, online reservations are highly recommended. The official website or local tourism offices provide the most accurate updates, and advanced booking is helpful, especially during tourist season.

The lighthouse is best reached on foot via the designated pedestrian route that starts near the Ferry Terminal. Sturdy walking shoes are recommended due to the distance and stairs. As one of Genoa's most iconic landmarks, the Lanterna offers not just a scenic view, but a powerful link between the city's seafaring past and its modern industrial port.

17. PALAZZO DI SAN GIORGIO

The Palazzo di San Giorgio is a remarkable architectural jewel that encapsulates centuries of the city's history. Constructed in the mid-1200s, the palace presents a captivating blend of Gothic and Renaissance styles. Its vibrant façade—decorated with colorful frescoes of Saint George slaying the dragon—immediately commands attention and reflects Genoa's enduring pride and symbolism. Once a powerful seat of civic governance and later home to the renowned Bank of Saint George, today it houses the Port Authority, continuing its role in Genoa's maritime legacy.

Visitors will appreciate the palace both for its structure and its rich iconography. The vivid external artwork, despite its age, continues to attract admirers and tells stories of Genoa's rise as a maritime republic. The architectural contrast between the older Gothic section and the more refined Renaissance additions, with one side facing the port and the other the inner city, speaks volumes about the adaptive evolution of the building through centuries of use and political change.

Although now functioning as an administrative center, the Palazzo often opens its ground floor to the public for temporary exhibits. These range from cultural showcases to contemporary art, offering a window into Genoa's creative life. Access to upper levels is typically restricted, but guided tours or special events sometimes permit further exploration. Checking the city's tourism website or visitor centers in advance is a good way to find out what's currently available for viewing.

Adding to its allure is the legend that Marco Polo was held prisoner here after a naval battle with the Genoese. It's believed that during his incarceration, he narrated his famous travels to a fellow inmate, creating the basis for The Travels of Marco Polo. Whether fully true or not, the tale adds a compelling global dimension to the palace's historical narrative and evokes thoughts of past figures who once inhabited its rooms.

Conveniently located near Genoa's historic port and old town, the Palazzo di San Giorgio is easily included in a walking tour of the city's heritage sites. Public transportation, including the nearby metro station, makes it accessible from various parts of Genoa. There is typically no fee to admire the exterior, though indoor exhibitions may have a small charge. Spring and early autumn are ideal for visits, with milder weather and the city's energy in full swing.

18. CHIESA DEL GESÙ E DEI SANTI AMBROGIO E ANDREA

The Chiesa del Gesù e dei Santi Ambrogio e Andrea, commonly known as the Church of the Gesù, is one of Genoa's most striking examples of Baroque religious architecture. Originally founded in the 500s and dedicated to Saint Ambrose, the church was completely redesigned by the Jesuits in the late 16th century. The current neoclassical façade, reconstructed in the 1800s and inspired by drawings from Rubens, sets the stage for the ornate magnificence found inside.

Once inside, visitors are met with a dazzling explosion of Baroque artistry. Marble columns, gilded surfaces, and expertly carved sculptures fill every corner. The richly decorated ceiling features vivid frescoes that draw the eye upward, offering a spiritual and visual experience. The church houses paintings by masters such as Rubens and Guido Reni, as well as native Genoese Baroque artists like the Carlone brothers, who contributed to the city's rich artistic legacy.

For tourists, this church is a prime destination not just for its religious importance, but for its cultural and aesthetic value. Each altar and chapel reveals complex craftsmanship, and the sheer variety of artworks demands a slow, thoughtful exploration. Since it remains an active place of worship, visitors are advised to be respectful, particularly during mass or special religious events. Opening hours may change during holidays or for restoration purposes, so confirming ahead of time is wise.

The church is within steps of major attractions like Palazzo Ducale and San Lorenzo Cathedral. Its proximity to Piazza De Ferrari means it's easy to include in any central sightseeing plan. After a visit, the surrounding square offers several cafés and benches for rest and reflection, making it a pleasant place to linger.

Visitors should allow at least an hour to fully take in the ornate interiors and artistic treasures. Flash photography is usually discouraged to preserve delicate artwork. Whether you're an art lover, a spiritual seeker, or someone who simply enjoys beautiful places, the Church of the Gesù offers a powerful experience of Genoa's religious and artistic soul.

19. VILLA DEL PRINCIPE

The Villa del Principe, also known as the Palace of Andrea Doria, stands as the grandest noble residence in Genoa. Commissioned in the early 1500s by the esteemed Admiral Andrea Doria, the villa was intended to display his status and serve as his luxurious retreat. Although modern developments like railways have altered its original waterfront setting, the villa retains much of its Renaissance elegance and continues to reflect Doria's vision of grandeur.

Inside, visitors are transported into a world of frescoed ceilings, antique furnishings, and priceless artworks. Among the highlights are the elaborate murals by Perino del Vaga, a pupil of Raphael, whose works such as the Fall of the Giants and Loggia degli Eroi celebrate classical myths and the Doria family legacy. Flemish tapestries from the 15th and 16th centuries, including scenes from the Battle of Lepanto, add further richness to the visual experience. Portraits and artifacts connected to the Doria Pamphilj lineage tell a story that spans several centuries.

The gardens, though smaller than they were in the villa's prime, have been faithfully restored to their original Renaissance layout. Visitors can stroll through paths lined with blooming flowers and aromatic herbs, eventually arriving at iconic features like the Dolphin Fountain by Perino del Vaga and the grand Neptune Fountain by Taddeo Carlone. The outdoor space complements the villa's interior opulence with natural beauty and classical design.

The villa is accessible by public transport, including the nearby Darsena metro station. It's typically open daily between 10:00 AM and 6:00 PM, but schedules can vary, so it's best to consult the official website before your visit. Purchasing tickets in advance, especially if you plan to tour both the house and gardens—is strongly recommended.

Visitors interested in history and art will benefit from guided tours, which offer rich insights into the Doria family, the artworks, and the villa's place in Genoese history. Photography is allowed (without flash), and weekdays are often less crowded for a more relaxed experience. For those seeking a luxurious and historically immersive outing, the Villa del Principe is not to be missed.

20. FORTE DIAMANTE

Forte Diamante, dramatically perched atop Monte Diamante at 667 meters, is one of Genoa's most commanding military relics. Constructed between 1756 and 1758 as part of the city's massive "New Walls" fortification system, the fort served as a northern stronghold, guarding key mountain passes. Though abandoned by the military in 1914 and currently closed to internal visitors, the exterior remains intact, drawing in hikers, photographers, and history enthusiasts seeking panoramic views and solitude.

The fort's isolated position offers some of the most breathtaking vistas in the region. From its summit, visitors can gaze across Genoa, the Ligurian Sea, and even glimpse Corsica on particularly clear days. Getting there involves a scenic and moderately challenging hike, with routes beginning in Righi, accessible via funicular from central Genoa, or the nearby hamlet of Trensasco via the narrow-gauge Casella railway line.

While you won't be able to explore the interior, the surrounding Parco delle Mura offers plenty of rewards. This greenbelt area is lined with trails, wildflowers, and old stone paths, making the journey to Forte Diamante a highlight in itself. Most hikers complete the round trip in three to four hours, depending on the route and individual pace. Be sure to pack suitable hiking gear, including good shoes, sun protection, and extra water, especially during warmer months.

Given its elevation and exposed terrain, weather conditions at the fort can be unpredictable. A light jacket is recommended even in summer, and visitors should monitor forecasts in advance. Though the hike is manageable for most, families with small children or mobility concerns should plan carefully, as the trail includes steeper sections and limited shelter.

The trail to Forte Diamante begins near Sentiero delle Mura, 16135 Genoa (Sant'Olcese area). There's no road access directly to the fort, which only adds to its allure. Combining military history with a challenging yet scenic walk, Forte Diamante makes for an unforgettable Genoese day hike.

21. FORTE BEGATO

Forte Begato is an impressive 19th-century fortress located high above Genoa's port area, built between 1818 and 1831 as part of the city's enhanced defense strategy under the Savoy rule. Designed to secure Genoa from northern threats, particularly through the Val Polcevera corridor, the fort once housed over 800 troops and large weapon reserves. Its later use as a wartime prison and military storage site adds depth to its historical significance.

Nowadays, the site offers visitors a fusion of nature and military history. The fortress is part of the larger Parco delle Mura—a sprawling green zone that contains Genoa's 17th-century defensive walls and other historic forts. Though the interior of Forte Begato is often inaccessible, the outer walls and surrounding plateau provide ample opportunity for scenic walks, quiet contemplation, and panoramic photo ops.

Reaching the fort involves either a bus ride (such as lines 35 or 36) or a moderately steep hike from central Genoa. On weekends and public holidays, access is often easier, and the grounds tend to be livelier with families, local hikers, and occasional guided tours. Shortly, a new cableway project promises even smoother access to the area from the city's Principe station.

Visitors are encouraged to wear appropriate footwear, bring a picnic, and carry a camera to capture the sweeping views of Genoa's skyline and harbor. While the grounds are generally well-maintained, parts of the fort show signs of wear, such as graffiti or scattered litter. Still, the atmosphere remains inviting, with local volunteers often involved in cleanup and event organization.

Whether as a short excursion or part of a full-day hike across multiple forts, it provides a satisfying experience for travelers interested in Genoa's military heritage and elevated vantage points.

22. FORTE CASTELLACCIO

Forte Castellaccio is a key piece of Genoa's extensive fortress system, situated in the elevated Righi district. This historic stronghold, once crucial to the city's military defense, now forms part of the vast Parco Urbano delle Mura. At its core is the distinctive Torre della Specola, a polygonal red-brick observatory tower that once fired a ceremonial cannon to mark the noon hour, a tradition rooted in Genoese timekeeping.

Though the interior of Forte Castellaccio is not always open to the public, the site remains popular for its stunning views and its inclusion in numerous hiking circuits. From its position atop Mount Peralto, visitors can take in far-reaching views across Genoa, the Ligurian coast, and the mountainous hinterland. The fort is often a featured stop on guided walking tours through the city's northern ridge.

Access to Forte Castellaccio is typically via the Zecca–Righi funicular, which provides a scenic ride up to the hilltop. From there, a series of trails lead visitors along the "New Walls" toward the fort. These paths can be rugged and steep in places, so comfortable hiking footwear and water are essential. While not overly technical, the terrain does require a reasonable level of fitness.

It's advisable to check the weather and plan the visit during the cooler parts of the day. On warm days, bring sun protection and refreshments, as there are no facilities near the fort itself. The site's appeal lies in its tranquility and its role as a gateway to Genoa's hilltop defenses, ideal for travelers seeking a mix of nature and history.

Forte Castellaccio is located in the Righi area, Genoa, Italy. Though it may not be fully open year-round, the panoramic hike and fortress backdrop provide a rewarding outing. For a deeper dive, consider combining it with stops at other nearby forts such as Sperone or Begato, making for a full-day outdoor adventure.

23. FORTE SPERONE

Perched atop Mount Peralto, Forte Sperone is a commanding fortress that forms a vital part of Genoa's historic "New Walls" defensive network. Its name, "Sperone" (spur), comes from its sharp, wedge-like shape where two walls meet, giving the impression of a ship's prow. The site's origins date to a 14th-century Ghibelline outpost, but the current structure is the result of significant military developments spanning the 17th to 19th centuries. Due to its elevated and strategic location, it played a central role in protecting the city and overseeing the surrounding valleys.

Forte Sperone is now open to visitors, offering a striking blend of historic architecture and scenic beauty. Entry to the complex is through a heavily fortified gate adorned with the coat of arms of the House of Savoy, once protected by a moat and a retractable bridge. Inside, you'll find multiple levels that once supported daily life for hundreds of troops, including storerooms, cisterns, and dormitories. These days, the fortress hosts occasional events, but most come to enjoy the peaceful setting and sweeping panoramic views of Genoa and the Ligurian coast.

Travelers interested in military history, engineering, or scenic walks will find much to admire here. As you explore, you'll encounter interpretive signs and displays recounting the fort's involvement in critical events such as the Austrian siege of 1747 and the 19th-century Risorgimento campaigns. The fort offers a vivid glimpse into the design and scale of Genoese fortifications and the evolving art of warfare.

Visitors should prepare for a bit of a climb, as reaching the site involves walking uphill. Sturdy shoes are essential due to uneven ground, and the elevated position means it can be breezy, so bringing a windbreaker or light jacket is wise. The views at the top, over city rooftops, coastal cliffs, and wooded hills—make the effort worthwhile and are ideal for photography or peaceful reflection.

Forte Sperone is accessible via the Metro (Dinegro station), bus line 35, or the scenic Zecca-Righi funicular followed by a walk. Some guided hikes include the fort as part of their route, making for a rewarding, historically rich day trip through Genoa's highlands.

24. PORTO ANTICO

Porto Antico, Genoa's revitalized Old Port, is a dynamic waterfront district that blends history, leisure, and culture. Once the beating heart of the Mediterranean trade, this massive area underwent a stunning transformation in the 1990s under the direction of acclaimed architect Renzo Piano. The result is a modern hub where past and present coexist, offering visitors and locals alike an energetic space full of attractions, dining, and scenic coastal views.

Among Porto Antico's top draws is the Acquario di Genova, one of Europe's largest aquariums, which offers a captivating look at marine life from around the world. Close by, visitors can take a ride on the Bigo panoramic lift for elevated city views or step into the Biosfera, a futuristic glass dome housing a miniature tropical ecosystem. These modern landmarks serve as both architectural icons and engaging attractions.

The area also thrives with repurposed industrial buildings like the Magazzini del Cotone, now home to museums, theaters, and family-oriented venues such as the Città dei Bambini. You'll also find the historic Porta Siberia gate and a broad promenade lined with restaurants, cafes, and gelato shops. It's an ideal spot for both cultural outings and casual relaxation by the water.

Easily reached on foot from Genoa's old town or via the metro (San Giorgio stop) and several bus lines, Porto Antico is a must-see for any visitor. Weekends and holidays can get busy, so plan for popular attractions. Combo tickets are available for multiple venues, which can help save money and time. As always in crowded public areas, keeping an eye on your belongings is advisable.

More than just a sightseeing district, Porto Antico regularly hosts festivals, concerts, and events like the Genoa Boat Show. Whether you're here for marine life, architecture, or simply a sunset stroll beside the sea, this vibrant district is one of the best ways to experience modern Genoa.

25. BIGO ELEVATOR

The Bigo panoramic elevator is a futuristic structure in Genoa's Porto Antico that offers one of the most dramatic views in the city. Designed by architect Renzo Piano for the 1992 Expo, the structure resembles an abstract crane or flower, symbolizing Genoa's historic maritime connections. The central feature—a rotating glass cabin—is suspended from one of the structure's limbs, lifting passengers high above the waterfront for an unforgettable aerial perspective.

The ride provides a calm, 360-degree rotation once the cabin reaches its peak at 40 meters above ground. Inside, you'll find multilingual audio guides and visual displays that point out Genoa's landmarks and offer interesting facts about its urban and maritime history. The journey is short but rich in both views and information, ideal for travelers seeking an overview of the city in minutes.

From this elevated vantage point, you can see the Old Port in full detail, the Biosfera, the Aquarium, and the city's maze-like medieval center. Further out, Forts and hills stretch into the distance, and iconic features like the San Lorenzo Cathedral and the Lanterna lighthouse come into view. It's a breathtaking, immersive way to orient yourself to the city's layout.

Tickets can be bought on-site, but during weekends and holidays, advance online booking is recommended. The Bigo isn't just a ride, it's a moving observatory that gives visitors an unparalleled glimpse into Genoa's beauty and complexity. Whether you're a photographer, a first-time visitor, or a local rediscovering your city, this lift offers an experience you won't soon forget.

26. EATALY

Eataly Genoa, nestled within the Porto Antico area, is a one-stop destination for lovers of Italian cuisine. Housed inside the striking Edificio Millo, this food emporium offers far more than a typical grocery store, it's a curated space where guests can eat, shop, and learn about Italy's rich culinary heritage. With floor-to-ceiling views of the harbor and a sleek, inviting interior, it's a must-visit for food enthusiasts and curious travelers alike.

Inside, the market overflows with high-quality products from across Italy. Visitors will find everything from fresh pasta and artisan cheeses to olive oils, truffles, sauces, and wine. There are casual food counters for quick snacks and full-service restaurants offering regional seafood dishes and Ligurian specialties like trofie al pesto. Dining with a view of Genoa's harbor adds to the charm.

One of Eataly's core missions is education. Informational signs, live demonstrations, and occasional cooking classes allow visitors to deepen their appreciation of Italian food culture. It's a space where watching a chef prepare your meal is part of the experience, and where questions about provenance and preparation are welcomed.

Given Eataly's popularity, try visiting during weekday afternoons for a more relaxed atmosphere. Dining reservations are recommended, especially for tables with a view. Don't hesitate to seek advice from staff, they're often knowledgeable and eager to guide you to the perfect product or pairing. Consider picking up culinary gifts like regional pasta or Ligurian wine for a unique souvenir.

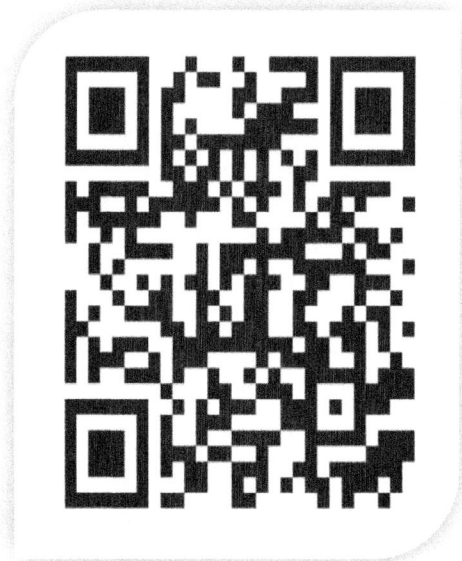

Eataly is conveniently positioned for anyone touring Porto Antico. While some products may carry premium prices, the authenticity, variety, and quality justify the experience. It's a rewarding stop whether you're seeking a full meal, a picnic treat, or inspiration for your next Italian dish.

27. AQUARIUM OF GENOA

The Aquarium of Genoa (Acquario di Genova) is one of Europe's largest and most popular aquariums, located in the heart of Porto Antico. Its seaside setting enhances the immersive experience, aligning perfectly with the city's strong nautical identity. Spanning multiple levels and home to over 12,000 animals across hundreds of species, it offers a compelling blend of education, conservation, and spectacle.

Inside, visitors journey through a variety of aquatic worlds, from tropical coral ecosystems to icy Antarctic habitats. Highlights include large tanks with sharks and rays, a dolphin pool, interactive jellyfish exhibits, and penguin colonies. Informational panels and audio-visual installations explain the biology and environmental needs of the animals, making the aquarium both entertaining and informative.

To make the most of your visit, plan, especially during weekends and holidays when crowds are common. Booking online is strongly advised, and arriving early or visiting later in the afternoon can help you avoid long lines. A visit typically lasts two to three hours, though there's enough to keep curious minds entertained for longer.

The aquarium also emphasizes marine conservation, often showcasing temporary exhibitions on ocean health, endangered species, and sustainable fishing. Check the official website for current offerings and seasonal events.

Photography is generally allowed, though flash is restricted in some areas. The Aquarium of Genoa is easy to reach from any part of the city, and an essential stop for families, nature lovers, and anyone fascinated by the underwater world.

28. BIOSFERA

The Biosfera in Genoa is a remarkable glass-and-steel dome situated in the city's Porto Antico district. Conceived by celebrated architect Renzo Piano and opened in 2001 for the G8 Summit, this structure, fondly called "La Bolla" (The Bubble), serves as a miniature tropical rainforest. Controlled by an advanced climate system, the Biosfera was created to raise awareness about the fragile ecosystems of tropical forests, which are rich in biodiversity yet under severe threat due to deforestation and climate change.

Inside, visitors are enveloped in a humid, warm environment that replicates rainforest conditions. More than 150 plant species flourish here, including rare tree ferns, banana and coffee plants, cinnamon trees, and rubber plants. The habitat also supports a selection of exotic animals such as scarlet ibises with vivid red feathers, white cockatoos, turtle doves, marsh turtles, and various tropical insects and fish. While compact in scale, the Biosfera offers an up-close and personal look at tropical biodiversity.

For those touring Genoa, this enclosed rainforest offers a short but enriching escape into nature. It's a great educational stop, especially for families, and its size makes it easy to explore in under half an hour. The exhibit emphasizes ecological preservation while surrounding visitors in a striking, futuristic space. Its distinctive structure and photogenic environment make it popular among tourists looking to combine learning with sightseeing.

Keep in mind that the interior climate mimics equatorial conditions, so light clothing is ideal. Hours of operation can vary seasonally, so checking ahead is advised. Many visitors choose to include the Biosfera as part of a combo ticket with the nearby Aquarium of Genoa, maximizing both time and value.

Though modest in size, it delivers a powerful message about sustainability. This innovative dome perfectly reflects Genoa's modern approach to combining architecture, education, and environmental responsibility in one captivating space.

29. LA CITTÀ DEI BAMBINI E DEI RAGAZZI

La Città dei Bambini e dei Ragazzi, translated as "The City of Children and Young People", is Genoa's premier hands-on museum for kids aged 2 to 13. Recently renovated and located beneath the Genoa Aquarium in Porto Antico, this interactive space is the first of its kind in Italy to focus on the five human senses. Far from a typical museum, it blends education with play, offering children an imaginative and technology-rich environment where they can explore their world through touch, sound, sight, taste, and smell.

Once inside, families are encouraged to roam freely. There's no set path, and over 40 interactive exhibits across 2,000 square meters invite young minds to play and discover at their own pace. Whether experimenting with light, sound, or construction, the activities are designed to match various developmental stages. Most visits last around two hours, but there's no time limit, so children can revisit their favorite exhibits and explore new ones as long as they like.

Special areas cater to toddlers aged 2 to 4, offering playful and safe zones like the "Playground Splash!" and "House in Construction."
These age-appropriate sections provide stimulating play while ensuring safety. Amenities such as baby-changing stations, lockers, and a refreshment area help make the visit comfortable for the entire family, ensuring both kids and adults have a smooth and enjoyable experience.

Visitors should note that while tickets are not named or personalized, booking is strongly suggested, especially on weekends or holidays. The entry includes timed slots, and the museum often sells out. Combined tickets with the Genoa Aquarium are available, offering an efficient way to see both attractions in one day. Be aware of entry rules: kids must

wear non-slip socks, and adults are required to wear overshoes, which are provided free or at a minimal fee.

The museum is situated conveniently in the Porto Antico zone. Easily accessible by public transit or a short walk from Genoa Piazza Principe Station, this family-friendly destination is a top choice for interactive, sensory-based fun.

30. GENOA'S 'CARUGGI'

The 'caruggi' is Genoa's famous narrow alleys, a maze-like network that forms the core of its medieval city center, one of the largest and most atmospheric in all of Europe. Originally designed for defense and efficient urban trade, these slender passages between tall buildings are a living remnant of the city's powerful maritime past. Walking through them feels like stepping into a different time, where each corner offers a surprise or a story waiting to be discovered.

Tourists will find the 'caruggi' rich with local flavor. Expect to stumble upon cozy food stalls selling traditional Ligurian fare, including freshly baked focaccia and farinata. Small artisan shops, hidden shrines, and noble palaces, many parts of the UNESCO-listed Palazzi dei Rolli, sit side by side with modest homes. This vibrant juxtaposition creates a compelling portrait of Genoa's social and architectural history.

These alleys remain lived-in and animated. Locals fill them with everyday life, from the chatter of markets to the aromas wafting out of family kitchens and trattorias. Because the streets can be uneven and winding, comfortable shoes are essential. While the area is generally safe, it's wise to stay aware of your surroundings, especially after dark, as some less-trafficked parts retain an edgy, authentic character.

Walking is the only real way to appreciate the 'caruggi'. Take time to look up, you'll notice ornate balconies, carved stone decorations, and glimpses of how Genoa once housed both merchant families and common workers side by side. Some of the best experiences come from veering off the main routes, where you'll find unexpected beauty and local spots untouched by tourist crowds.

Centered between landmarks like Piazza De Ferrari, Porto Antico, and the train station at Piazza Principe, the 'caruggi' stretch across neighborhoods like Prè,

Maddalena, and Molo. Start your wander around the Old Port or the Doge's Palace, and let the alleys lead you on a memorable urban adventure.

31. PIAZZA DE FERRARI

Piazza De Ferrari is Genoa's central square and the beating heart of city life, where historic splendor meets modern-day bustle. With its irregular layout, a product of early 20th-century urban unification, this square is instantly recognizable thanks to its grand bronze fountain at the center. Installed in 1936, the fountain adds dramatic flair with its cascading jets, especially striking when illuminated at night.

Around the square, visitors are surrounded by architectural treasures. The elegant Palazzo della Borsa showcases Genoese Art Nouveau design, while the Teatro Carlo Felice, home to the city's opera, adds neoclassical prestige. The entrance to the Palazzo Ducale (Doge's Palace) faces the square, linking this lively space to Genoa's powerful past as a republic. Together, these landmarks make the piazza an ideal launch point for exploring the city.

For tourists, the square is perfect for a break between attractions. The area is largely pedestrianized, offering a pleasant space to roam freely. Fashion lovers will appreciate nearby streets like Via Roma and Via XX Settembre, which offer a mix of luxury boutiques and high-street shops.

Piazza De Ferrari is also a vital transit node. The De Ferrari metro stop is directly on the square, and bus lines fan out in every direction. The piazza also opens directly into the narrow alleyways of the historic center, making it easy to continue exploring on foot.

For the best experience, consider visiting both during the day and in the evening. The lighting after dusk offers a whole new perspective. With local restaurants and cultural institutions just steps away, this square remains a must-visit part of Genoa's urban charm.

32. PIAZZA DELLE ERBE

Nestled in Genoa's historic district, Piazza delle Erbe is a beloved square that combines medieval character with vibrant modern energy. Once a bustling market for herbs and vegetables—hence its name—the piazza now thrives as a lively meeting spot surrounded by colorful buildings, small bars, and cozy cafés. Cobblestone streets and historic facades make it one of the city's most photogenic spots, perfect for soaking in local life.

In the morning, especially during market days, the square buzzes with vendors offering fresh produce and handmade goods. It's an ideal time to experience local culture up close. As the day progresses, the piazza shifts into a laid-back atmosphere. Outdoor tables appear, and visitors can sip espresso or enjoy a light lunch while watching the comings and goings of daily life.

By nightfall, Piazza delle Erbe transforms yet again. It becomes a vibrant hub of nightlife, with bars filling up and music spilling into the square. Locals and tourists gather to enjoy cocktails, conversations, and the electric energy that pulses through this part of the old town. On weekends, the area stays lively well into the night, making it a favorite hangout for younger crowds and nightlife enthusiasts.

The piazza is located in Genoa's Centro Storico, just a short walk from landmarks such as Piazza De Ferrari, the Doge's Palace, and Porta Soprana. It's easily accessible on foot or via metro (De Ferrari stop) and buses. Be sure to wear comfortable shoes—the cobbled surfaces and slight slopes are charming but not always easy on the feet.

Whether you visit by day for the markets or by night for the lively crowd, Piazza delle Erbe offers

a

full spectrum of Genoese charm. With its dynamic pace and historic setting, this square promises a rich, sensory-filled experience for every traveler.

33. CHIESA DI SAN MATTEO

Tucked within the medieval Piazza San Matteo, the Chiesa di San Matteo is one of Genoa's most historically significant churches, closely tied to the powerful Doria family. Found at Piazza S. Matteo 18, 16123 Genova, the church's signature black-and-white striped façade, complete with arched windows and a central rose window, exemplifies Genoese Gothic style. Divided by three ornamental columns, the structure also reflects Renaissance additions, blending centuries of artistic trends into one harmonious design.

Inside, the church presents a contrast to its austere exterior. The interiors were renovated in the 1500s at Andrea Doria's request and now feature refined Renaissance embellishments. Visitors can admire frescoes by artists like Luca Cambiaso and Giovanni Battista Castello, stucco work, paintings, and complexly carved wooden sculptures by Anton Maria Maragliano. This meeting of Gothic structure and Renaissance detail creates a distinctive, layered aesthetic experience.

The crypt, located beneath the altar, is one of the church's most compelling features. It contains the tomb of Admiral Andrea Doria, adorned with elaborate statues and marble reliefs crafted by Giovanni Angelo Montorsoli. Also displayed is Doria's sword—a tangible link to his military past. Sacred relics from saints Pelagius and Maximus are interred here as well, along with a Baroque pipe organ by Antonio Alari, emphasizing the church's artistic and spiritual importance.

Beyond the church itself, the surrounding square enhances the experience. Raised above street level, Piazza San Matteo is ringed with Gothic-style Doria family residences, their facades echoing the church's black-and-white motif. From the left side of the church, visitors can access a cloister dating back to the 14th

century, a serene space featuring elegant arches and columns, ideal for quiet reflection away from the city's bustle.

A visit to Chiesa di San Matteo offers a window into Genoa's religious, architectural, and noble heritage. Allocate time to explore both the church and its setting in detail. Comfortable footwear is advisable for navigating Genoa's narrow alleyways. Respectful attire is recommended since it remains a functioning place of worship. Early visits typically offer a quieter, more contemplative experience at this deeply historical site.

34. PORTA SOPRANA

Porta Soprana, known as the "Upper Gate," is one of Genoa's most iconic medieval structures, serving as a key entrance to the city during the 12th century. Featuring two striking towers flanking a central stone archway, the gate is a rare survivor of Genoa's ancient defensive walls. Although much of the surrounding fortifications have disappeared due to urban growth, Porta Soprana still stands tall as a proud reminder of the city's Romanesque military heritage and its past as a powerful maritime republic.

Visitors to Porta Soprana can enjoy a genuine immersion in history. Just beside the gate lies the house believed to be Christopher Columbus's childhood home, adding even more historical resonance to the area. In some instances, the gate's interior spaces are open to the public, allowing a closer look at the stonework and inner chambers. Whether or not interior access is available, the gate and its surroundings make for a scenic and informative stroll, ideal for photography and for gaining a deeper appreciation of Genoa's layered past.

Today, Porta Soprana is set against a modern urban backdrop, and travelers should expect it to be nestled within a busy section of the city. Comfortable footwear is advised, as exploring the area involves a fair amount of walking. Information panels around the site often explain its history, enhancing the visit. As with any popular tourist site, it's wise to remain aware of personal belongings and to plan for some foot traffic, particularly during holidays and peak travel seasons.

One of the most engaging aspects of Porta Soprana is imagining the generations of travelers, merchants, and soldiers who once passed through this gateway. Its sheer height and solid construction demonstrate its once-crucial role in city defense. If accessible, elevated views from the towers offer a fresh perspective on Genoa's surrounding neighborhoods, contrasting ancient architecture with modern city life.

The changing daylight casts dramatic shadows on the gate, making it especially photogenic in the early morning or late afternoon.

The gate sits within walking distance of many key landmarks, including Piazza De Ferrari and the historic center. Its accessibility by public transport makes it an easy stop, and the proximity to the Columbus House and narrow alleyways gives travelers a rich, compact cultural experience. Plan a bit of extra time to fully appreciate both the gate and its storied surroundings.

35. CASTELLO MACKENZIE

Castello Mackenzie is a striking example of Neo-Gothic style in Genoa, designed by architect Gino Coppedè for Scottish insurance magnate Evan Mackenzie. Built between 1893 and 1905, this romantic fortress-like mansion is an architectural collage of Gothic, medieval, and Renaissance elements, echoing Mackenzie's passion for historical motifs. Lavish features include carved woodwork, painted ceilings, stained glass, and even an indoor swimming pool, all cleverly wrapped in a design that resembles a fairy-tale castle.

Today, the castle functions as a venue for cultural events, art exhibits, and auctions, primarily run by Cambi Auction House. The interior spaces, although sometimes occupied by event installations or auction pieces, still offer plenty to admire. One of the highlights is the castle's small chapel, richly decorated in a style that mirrors early Renaissance religious aesthetics. The mansion once housed an impressive private library, including a large collection of rare works dedicated to Dante Alighieri.

Castello Mackenzie is located in the Castelletto district, an elevated area with scenic views over Genoa and the coastline. Driving there can be tricky due to narrow, winding streets, so it's often easier to use public transit. Bus lines 34, 36, and 49, or a nearby funicular, provide easy access. As public access may depend on events, it's best to check the official website or contact tourist information services for current visiting hours and special programs. Guided tours are occasionally offered and are highly recommended for deeper context.

Walking through the castle is like stepping into a theatrical, imaginative space. The entrance hall, adorned with decorative ironwork, leads into grand halls filled with artistic flourishes. While not a traditional museum, the experience is immersive and personal—perfect for those with an appreciation for bold, eccentric architecture. If walking from the center, prepare for some uphill trekking, but the panoramic vistas and rich design are more than worth the effort.

Be sure to look closely at the finer details, from elaborate wood panels to symbolic carvings. The castle's history includes various uses, from a private home to military headquarters, and today, it functions as a vibrant cultural venue. Rather than a static monument, Castello Mackenzie is alive with changing exhibits and artistic energy, offering a distinctive Genoese experience far different from typical historic sites.

36. BASILICA DELLA SANTISSIMA ANNUNZIATA DEL VASTATO

The Basilica della Santissima Annunziata del Vastato is one of Genoa's most splendid sacred buildings, rich in late Mannerist and Baroque style. Construction began in 1520 by Franciscan friars and was later transformed during the 17th century under the generous patronage of the Lomellini family. Though the basilica suffered damage during World War II, many of its structural and decorative features survived, revealing a powerful blend of medieval and Baroque elements. Among them are the original black-and-white stone columns, contrasting with the interior's dazzling embellishments.

Inside, the basilica is a sensory marvel. Visitors are met with grand gold-covered ceilings, ornate stucco detailing, and richly painted frescoes throughout the nave and dome. Major Italian artists, including Guercino, Luca Cambiaso, and Giovanni Battista Carlone, contributed to its visual feast. A standout feature is the recently restored Last Supper by Giulio Cesare Procaccini, spanning 40 square meters and now fully visible in its vibrant original form.

The atmosphere within the basilica is both majestic and contemplative. Towering marble columns and a dramatic central dome create an awe-inspiring space for reflection and admiration. Even literary figures like Charles Dickens were struck by the building's splendor, marveling at the luminous effect of gold that dances in the sunlight. Visitors can experience the same enchantment and reverence that captivated writers and travelers centuries ago.

Entry is typically free, and small guidebooks are available for those interested in learning more about the basilica's artistic and historical context. Modest dress is advised, as this remains an active place of worship. To avoid crowds and appreciate the basilica's finer details, try visiting early in the day or during weekdays. Self-guided exploration is rewarding, though guided tours can provide a deeper understanding of the site's significance and design.

You'll find the basilica at Piazza della Nunziata 4, in Genoa's historic center. It's easily accessible by foot and close to other attractions like the Palazzo Reale and Darsena metro stop. Whether you're drawn by religious interest, architectural beauty, or the allure of Italian art, this basilica is an essential destination within Genoa's old town.

37. CHURCH OF SANT'ANTONIO ABATE

Genoa is home to several churches named after Saint Anthony the Abbot, but two stand out: the Oratorio di Sant'Antonio Abate in the city center and the Chiesa di Sant'Antonio Abate in Pegli. Though they share a name, their settings and atmospheres are quite different. The oratory, located in the ancient Molo district, sits amid Genoa's dense historic core, while the Pegli church lies in a quieter seaside suburb. Both reflect Genoa's rich ecclesiastical tradition but in unique ways.

The Oratorio di Sant'Antonio Abate in the Molo district is tucked into a web of narrow medieval streets, part of a UNESCO World Heritage area. It blends into the layered cityscape, built around or atop older structures. Modest in appearance, the oratory still holds cultural importance, revealing traces of Genoa's religious evolution over centuries. Its intimate scale contrasts with the grandeur of other city churches but offers a more personal encounter with Genoese faith traditions.

Visiting the oratory means navigating Genoa's famous "caruggi," the labyrinthine alleys of the old town. These alleyways, though atmospheric and historic, can be a bit dim or confusing, so sensible walking shoes and daytime visits are recommended. The journey is half the experience—each turn can reveal hidden chapels, artisan shops, or local bakeries offering Genoese specialties. Awareness of the surroundings, especially at night, ensures a safe and rewarding visit.

The Pegli counterpart, located at Via Caldesi 8, provides a more peaceful setting. Pegli is a seaside district with a residential feel, perfect for a calmer, less crowded experience. While the church doesn't boast the same architectural prominence or fame, it represents everyday religious life in modern Genoa. It's ideal for travelers wanting to escape the hustle of the center and enjoy a reflective, neighborhood experience.

Whether visiting the Oratorio in the historic heart or the Chiesa in the coastal Pegli district, both churches offer insight into Genoa's devotional life. Respectful conduct is encouraged, especially during services. Each location, in its way, connects you to the rhythms of Genoese spirituality, one through the pulse of the ancient city, the other through serene, local tradition.

38. CHURCH OF SAN DONATO

Tucked into the twisting lanes of Genoa's Old Town, the Church of San Donato stands as a beautiful example of Romanesque architecture dating back to the 12th century. Its stone façade and distinctive octagonal bell tower stand out against the colorful buildings nearby. Though more modest than the city's cathedrals, San Donato captures the essence of Genoa's medieval identity, inviting visitors into a world where history and spiritual devotion converge.

A step inside San Donato reveals a rich collection of sacred art and architecture. Highlights include paintings by renowned Genoese artists like Bernardo Castello and Domenico Piola, as well as ornate sculptures and altarpieces. One of the most treasured pieces is the "Adoration of the Magi" triptych by Joos van Cleve, a 16th-century Flemish master. This singular work adds to the church's reputation as a quiet yet important cultural destination.

San Donato's preservation is notable, considering Genoa's turbulent urban development and war history. The Romanesque architecture remains remarkably intact, offering a serene interior space for reflection. Take time to admire the details—from carved columns to decorative chapels—that tell the story of the church's enduring place in Genoa's religious landscape.

The surrounding district is equally captivating. Located in Europe's largest medieval old town, the church sits among "caruggi" packed with artisan shops, bakeries, and quiet courtyards. Exploring on foot is essential, and sturdy shoes are recommended for the cobbled terrain. This area offers a mix of gritty authenticity and quiet charm, perfect for those seeking more than just the typical tourist trail.

Located at Via S. Donato 10, 16123 Genoa, the church is close to many attractions like Piazza De Ferrari and the Old Port. It's easily included in a walking tour of the historic center. While generally safe during the day, some alleyways can feel a bit desolate at night, so daytime visits are preferred. For travelers looking to discover the hidden gems of Genoa, San Donato delivers a memorable and enriching experience.

39. PALAZZO DELLA MERIDIANA

The Palazzo della Meridiana, also referred to as Palazzo Gerolamo Grimaldi, is a refined 16th-century residence that highlights Genoa's architectural evolution during the Renaissance period. Commissioned by the affluent banker Gerolamo Grimaldi Oliva between 1536 and 1544, the palace is a distinguished member of the "Palazzi dei Rolli" – a network of noble estates designated for hosting visiting dignitaries in the time of the Genoese Republic. The building's moniker, "della Meridiana," originates from a sundial painted on the façade in the 1700s, a charming detail that sets it apart visually and symbolically.

Today, the palace functions as a dynamic cultural space, frequently hosting exhibitions, artistic events, and private receptions. Although still under private ownership, it opens periodically to the public, especially during cultural festivals or designated visiting days. The palace's interior impresses with a striking fusion of styles spanning multiple centuries. Visitors can admire remarkable frescoes by famed artists such as Luca Cambiaso and Giovanni Battista Castello, alongside 20th-century Art Nouveau rooms designed by Gino Coppedè, which add a unique layer of visual interest.

Tourists should be aware that public access is not guaranteed daily. It is essential to consult the official website or local listings for current event schedules or opportunities to join guided tours. As a UNESCO-recognized landmark within the Rolli palaces, a visit here provides a rare chance to appreciate the decorative opulence and architectural innovation that once impressed European royalty and ambassadors during their Genoese stays.

Inside the palace, visitors are encouraged to seek out specific highlights such as the "Labours of Hercules" series attributed to Aurelio Busso and Luca Cambiaso's narrative fresco of Ulysses, known for its masterful use of spatial illusion. The juxtaposition of Renaissance symmetry, Baroque grandeur, and Art Nouveau flair creates a fascinating progression of artistic trends under one roof. The high ceilings, detailed wall panels, and graceful arches speak to the splendor of Genoese aristocracy.

Located at Salita San Francesco, 4, in Genoa's historic core, Palazzo della Meridiana is ideally situated for those already exploring the Palazzi dei Rolli trail. Given the building's infrequent public hours, visitors are encouraged to combine it with nearby attractions and guided city tours. A stop here offers not only architectural beauty but also an authentic window into the city's noble past.

40. CARLO FELICE THEATRE

The Teatro Carlo Felice stands as Genoa's main opera venue and an architectural landmark that blends 19th-century grandeur with modern design. Originally built in 1827, the theater was largely destroyed during World War II and later reconstructed with contemporary elements while retaining some of its neoclassical elegance. Located beside Piazza De Ferrari, the city's central square, it now serves as a cultural epicenter for operas, ballets, classical concerts, and international artistic performances.

Audiences entering Teatro Carlo Felice will find a spacious hall designed to resemble an open-air piazza, with stylized façades along the walls and a ceiling illuminated with star-like lights. This distinctive interior merges theatrical tradition with artistic innovation, creating an ambiance that enhances every performance. With seating for up to 2,000 and acoustics praised by performers and critics alike, the venue provides a top-tier experience for both seasoned patrons and first-time attendees.

Behind its refined setting lies a technologically advanced stage system, including a 63-meter scenic tower and multiple adjustable stages operated by computerized controls. These state-of-the-art features enable complex set changes and high-caliber productions. Visitors can also explore the unique 400-square-meter indoor plaza connecting Galleria Mazzini with Piazza De Ferrari, functioning as a stylish, glass-covered foyer.

To make the most of a visit, check the theater's programming via its official website. From Verdi operas to contemporary choreographies and international symphonies, the calendar appeals to a broad range of tastes. The box office is usually open Tuesday through Saturday, with extended hours on

performance evenings. Advance ticket reservations are recommended, particularly for popular events or seasonal galas.

On occasion, the theater hosts architectural and historical tours that guide visitors through backstage areas, highlighting its modern capabilities and storied past. Located in the heart of Genoa, Teatro Carlo Felice is within walking distance of other major attractions like Palazzo Ducale, making it a seamless addition to a day of cultural exploration.

Bonus Section: Customizable Itinerary Templates

As a special addition to this travel guide, this bonus section provides ready-to-use itinerary templates designed to help you plan your perfect Genoa adventure. These flexible outlines are meant to complement the suggestions found throughout this book while allowing you to modify and tailor your experience based on your interests, pace, and trip duration.

Whether you're visiting for a weekend, a full week, or simply looking to prioritize specific themes like history, food, or family-friendly activities, these templates will help you organize your journey with ease and confidence.

To access and download the full set of customizable itineraries for your personal use, scan the QR code. It will take you to a secure folder containing printable and editable formats.

Enjoy planning, and most importantly, enjoy Genoa your way!

CHAPTER 6: GENOA'S FOOD CULTURE & NIGHTLIFE

Must-Try Local Dishes

Genoa's unique geography has profoundly shaped its gastronomic identity, giving rise to a cuisine that is both simple and extraordinarily flavorful. "Ligurian Delights" is indeed a testament to this, boasting iconic dishes like pesto and focaccia that have captivated palates worldwide. But to truly appreciate Genoa's culinary heart, one must venture beyond these well-known stars and explore the constellation of other must-try local dishes.

At the very pinnacle of Ligurian cuisine stands Pesto alla Genovese. This vibrant green sauce, a symbol of Genoa itself, is far more than just a condiment; it's a testament to the region's dedication to fresh, high-quality ingredients. The magic of authentic pesto lies in its simplicity: Genovese basil (preferably young, tender leaves from Prà), pine nuts, garlic (often a milder variety), Pecorino Sardo and Parmigiano Reggiano cheeses, coarse sea salt, and the cornerstone – exquisite Ligurian extra virgin olive oil.

Traditionally, these ingredients are pounded in a marble mortar with a wooden pestle, a method that gently bruises the basil leaves, releasing their essential oils and preserving their delicate aroma, unlike the harsh blade of a food processor. The result is a fragrant, emerald-green sauce with a creamy texture and an explosion of herbaceous, nutty, and savory notes. While most commonly associated with trenette or trofie pasta, pesto is also divine with minestrone, spread on bruschetta, or even dolloped onto boiled potatoes and green beans, creating a harmonious and utterly satisfying meal. The very act of preparing pesto is a ritual, passed down through generations, ensuring the preservation of this culinary masterpiece.

Equally renowned and perhaps even more ubiquitous in daily Ligurian life is Focaccia, particularly Focaccia Genovese. This flatbread, golden and glistening with olive oil, is a staple at any time of day – for breakfast dipped in cappuccino (a uniquely Genovese custom), as a mid-morning snack, alongside lunch, or as an aperitivo. Unlike its thinner counterparts found elsewhere, Genovese focaccia is characterized by its soft, airy interior and a delightfully crisp, dimpled crust. These dimples, pressed into the dough before baking, are designed to catch pools of olive oil and coarse sea salt, intensifying its flavor. The dough itself is simple: flour, water, yeast, salt, and olive oil, but the secret lies in the long fermentation and precise hydration, which give it its characteristic light texture.

Beyond the classic focaccia con l'olio (with oil), variations abound, including focaccia con le cipolle (with onions), focaccia con le olive (with olives), and focaccia al formaggio (with cheese), a specialty of Recco, a town near Genoa, which features two paper-thin layers of dough encasing a rich, melted Stracchino cheese filling.

While pesto and focaccia reign supreme, the true depth of Ligurian cuisine is revealed in its lesser-known, yet equally delightful, dishes. Farinata is one such treasure. This savory pancake, made from chickpea flour, water, olive oil, and salt, is baked in a blistering hot wood-fired oven until it develops a golden, slightly crispy top and a creamy interior. Simple yet profoundly satisfying, farinata is naturally gluten-free and vegan, making it a popular choice. It's often enjoyed plain, seasoned only with black pepper, or sometimes topped with onions or rosemary. You'll find it sold by the slice in friggitorie (fried food shops) or bakeries, a perfect quick bite on the go.

Another quintessential Ligurian dish is Torta Pasqualina. While traditionally prepared for Easter (Pasqua), this savory pie is enjoyed year-round. It's a culinary marvel, featuring numerous (often 33, in homage to the age of Christ) delicate layers of paper-thin pastry, encasing a rich filling of Swiss chard or spinach, ricotta cheese, eggs, and often fresh marjoram. The eggs are sometimes cracked directly into hollows in the filling before baking, creating beautiful, perfectly cooked yolks within the slice. Torta Pasqualina exemplifies the Ligurian approach to cooking: making the most of humble ingredients to create something truly elegant and flavorful.

Given Genoa's strong maritime heritage, fish and seafood naturally play a significant role in its cuisine. Cappon Magro is perhaps the most elaborate and visually stunning of these dishes. More of an architectural masterpiece than a simple salad, it's a pyramid of boiled vegetables (potatoes, carrots, green beans, beetroot), hard-boiled eggs, seafood (often prawns, lobster, mussels, or white fish), and gallette del marinaio (a type of hardtack biscuit), all artfully arranged and generously dressed with a rich green sauce made from parsley, garlic, capers, anchovies, and olive oil. Historically a dish of the poor, made from leftover fish and vegetables, it evolved into an opulent celebratory dish, showcasing the abundance of the sea and land.

For those seeking a hearty, comforting meal, Minestrone alla Genovese is a must-try. Unlike other regional minestrones, the Genovese version is characterized by its inclusion of pesto, which is stirred into the soup just before serving, imparting its unique freshness and depth of flavor. It's a thick, vegetable-laden soup, typically featuring a medley of seasonal vegetables like potatoes, zucchini, green beans, peas, carrots, and sometimes pasta or rice, all simmered in a savory broth.

No exploration of Ligurian delights would be complete without mentioning the charming small pasta shapes, often served with pesto or other light sauces. Trofie, small, twisted pasta shapes that are perfect for capturing and holding sauce, are a local favorite. So too is trenette, a flat, narrow pasta similar to linguine, frequently served with pesto, potatoes, and green beans (a classic Ligurian combination known as trenette al pesto con patate e fagiolini).

Finally, for something sweet, Pandolce Genovese is the regional Christmas cake, though readily available in bakeries throughout the year. This dense, slightly crumbly sweet bread is studded with candied fruits, pine nuts, and raisins, flavored with fennel seeds and orange zest. There are two main versions: pandolce alto (tall), a yeast-leavened bread that rises slowly, and pandolce basso (short), a quicker-to-prepare, crumbly version more akin to a scone. Both offer a delightful end to a Ligurian meal.

Genoa's culinary landscape is a testament to its resourcefulness, its love for fresh, local ingredients, and its deep-rooted traditions. From the world-famous pesto and focaccia to the lesser-known but equally captivating farinata, torta pasqualina, and cappon magro, each dish tells a story of the land and the sea.

Genoa Nightlife

Genoa truly comes alive when the sun sets. From the ancient labyrinthine "caruggi" of the historic center to the modern allure of Porto Antico and the charming coastal villages, Genoa offers a diverse and engaging nightlife scene that caters to every taste. Whether you're seeking sophisticated cocktails, lively aperitivo, or vibrant waterfront entertainment, this Ligurian capital has something unique to offer.

The Allure of Aperitivo

No discussion of Italian nightlife is complete without a deep dive into the beloved tradition of aperitivo. In Genoa, this pre-dinner ritual is a cornerstone of social life, a time to unwind, socialize, and whet the appetite with drinks and complimentary snacks. Typically kicking off around 6 PM, aperitivo in Genoa is more than just a drink; it's a culinary and cultural experience.

Many bars throughout the city embrace the aperitivo concept, offering a generous spread of small bites alongside your chosen beverage. This can range from simple olives and focaccia to more elaborate buffets featuring local cured meats, cheeses, mini pizzas, and even pasta dishes. It's often so substantial that it can effectively serve as a light dinner, making it a budget-friendly way to enjoy the local flavors.

Key Aperitivo Hotspots:

1. Piazza delle Erbe: Nestled just below the grand Piazza De Ferrari, this quaint square transforms into a buzzing hub as evening approaches. Several bars here spill their tables onto the piazza, creating a lively atmosphere. It's particularly popular with a younger crowd, especially on Fridays, and offers a selection of bars like 28Erbe, Gradisca, Biggie, and Bar Berto, all offering excellent aperitivo.

2. Piazza Lavagna: For a slightly more mature and calmer ambiance, Piazza Lavagna is a charming choice. This spacious square, a welcome contrast to the narrow alleys, is home to venues like GloGlo Bistrot and Exultate, where you can enjoy a glass of Ligurian wine and focaccia in tranquility.

3. Porto Antico (Old Port): The redeveloped Porto Antico is a prime location for a sophisticated waterfront aperitivo. With its stunning views of the harbor and the iconic Lanterna, you'll find numerous trendy bars and restaurants offering elegant spreads. Places like La Goletta Seaside Pub and Banano Tsunami are perfect for enjoying a drink with a scenic backdrop.

4. Boccadasse: This picturesque old fishing village, with its pastel-colored houses clinging to the coastline, offers a magical setting for an aperitivo by the sea. While the aperitivo spread might be simpler here, the breathtaking sunset views from places like La Strambata make it an unforgettable experience.

When indulging in aperitivo, be sure to try a local Ligurian white wine or a "baxeichito," Genoa's signature cocktail made with basil – a refreshing and uniquely Genovese concoction.

Bars and Pubs

Genoa's bar scene is as varied as its cityscape, ranging from traditional taverns hidden within medieval alleys to sleek, modern cocktail lounges.

Historic Center's Hidden Gems:

The caruggi (narrow alleys) of Genoa's historic center are teeming with character and offer an authentic Genovese drinking experience. Here, you'll find a mix of cozy pubs and wine bars where locals enjoy their drinks, often spilling out into the streets.

1. Taverna Zaccaria: This cozy pub in the old town blends medieval charm with modern vibes, offering a unique setting near St. Cosma.

2. Britannia Pub: A traditional English pub located in Vico della Casana, offering a warm atmosphere and an excellent selection of beers, including Irish varieties like Kilkenny, alongside tasty burgers.

3. La Goccia Chupiteria: If you're looking for a fun night and an extensive list of cheap, colorful chupiti (shots), this bar in the narrow alleys is a local favorite.

4. Cantine Matteotti: A charming wine bar tucked away in the historic center, offering a balance of relaxation and sophistication.

5. Les Rouges Cucina & Cocktails: Housed in a 16th-century palace, this spot offers a unique atmosphere with exclusive cocktails and delicious Ligurian specialties.

Beyond the Caruggi:

As you venture beyond the densest parts of the old town, you'll discover different facets of Genoa's bar scene.

1. Piazza De Ferrari and Palazzo Ducale area: This central area boasts more elegant establishments, including classy wine bars serving fine Ligurian wines paired with local products, as well as chic lounge bars.

2. Malkovich Cocktail Bar: Known for its great cocktail selections and unique museum-like interior.

3. Mua Lounge: A super modern and contemporary cocktail bar near Piazza Ferrari, offering sleek white leather couches and an extensive cocktail menu.

Waterfront Entertainment: Dance, Music, and Scenic Views

Genoa's strong connection to the sea is reflected in its vibrant waterfront entertainment, especially prominent in the summer months. The Porto Antico and the promenade along Corso Italia offer a dynamic mix of clubs, bars, and venues with stunning sea views.

1. Porto Antico: This redeveloped area is not just for aperitivo; it transforms into a lively nightlife destination.

2. Banano Tsunami: Located directly on the water, this club boasts a fantastic location for dancing the night away, especially popular for weekend crowds and Erasmus parties on Wednesdays.

3. La Goletta Seaside Pub: Overlooking the Porto Antico, this charming establishment offers breathtaking views and a lively atmosphere.

The Porto Antico also hosts various events at the Piazzale delle Feste, including festivals like the Genova Hip Hop Festival.

- Corso Italia and Boccadasse: This picturesque promenade stretching east from the city center is a popular spot for evening strolls and leads to the enchanting village of Boccadasse.
- Mako Discotheque: Situated on Corso Italia, Mako is a three-in-one venue with an elegant cocktail bar, restaurant, and nightclub, playing "easy house," R&B, and revival music.

Live Music and Cultural Venues

Genoa's nightlife also caters to music enthusiasts with various venues offering live performances across different genres.

1. Jazz Clubs: For those who prefer a calmer environment and the soothing sounds of jazz and blues, Genoa has several intimate venues.

2. Count Basie Jazz Club: An essential gathering place for jazz lovers, offering an intimate and charming atmosphere.

3. Clubs and Discos: While some larger clubs are located outside the historic center along the Ligurian Riviera, there are options for dancing within or near the city.

4. Cezanne Disco: A historic club near Fiera di Genoa, catering to a more mature crowd with a mix of 80s music, Latin beats, and more (open Fridays and weekends).

5. Casa Mia Club and Mantra Club are known for electronic music events.

6. Palazzo Ducale: This historic palace occasionally hosts cultural events and even silent discos, offering a unique dance experience under the stars.

Planning Your Night Out in Genoa

1. Timing: Bars and aperitivo spots generally start getting crowded around 6 PM, especially on weekends and in summer. Dinner typically follows later, around 8 PM or 9 PM, with clubs usually kicking off around 11 PM or midnight.

2. Areas to Explore: The historic center (around Piazza delle Erbe, Piazza Lavagna, and the caruggi) is excellent for traditional bars, aperitivo, and a more intimate atmosphere. The Porto Antico and Corso Italia/Boccadasse areas are ideal for waterfront views, trendy clubs, and a more vibrant, dance-oriented scene, particularly in warmer months.

3. Local Drinks to Try: Beyond the classic Aperol Spritz, be sure to sample Ligurian white wines, the unique "baxeichito" (basil cocktail), and local craft beers.

4. Getting Around: The historic center is best explored on foot. For areas further afield like Corso Italia or Boccadasse, public transport (buses) or taxis are convenient options.

Genoa's nightlife offers a captivating blend of old-world charm and modern vibrancy. From the relaxed elegance of an aperitivo overlooking the sea to dancing the night away in a waterfront club or discovering a hidden gem in a medieval alley, the city invites you to immerse yourself in its nocturnal rhythm. No matter your preference, Genoa promises an unforgettable evening experience that beautifully complements its rich culture.

Local Markets & Food Streets

Genoa is a sensory feast, especially when it comes to its local markets and food streets. These vibrant hubs are not merely places of commerce; they are living testaments to Genoese culture, history, and a culinary tradition deeply rooted in fresh, local produce and the ingenuity of its people. Among the most iconic of these gastronomic havens are the Mercato Orientale and Via XX Settembre, each offering a distinct yet equally captivating glimpse into the heart of Genoese life.

Mercato Orientale

The Mercato Orientale, or Eastern Market, is a true landmark of Genoa, an architectural marvel that seamlessly blends historical grandeur with the bustling energy of a modern marketplace. Housed within a former convent, the market's stately facade on Via XX Settembre gives way to an expansive, airy interior where light filters through high windows, illuminating a kaleidoscope of colors and a symphony of sounds and aromas.

Stepping into the Mercato Orientale is like entering a parallel universe, a microcosm of Ligurian bounty. The sheer variety of goods on offer is staggering. Rows upon rows of stalls overflow with vibrant, seasonal fruits and vegetables, many of which are locally sourced from the fertile valleys surrounding Genoa. Here, you'll find the glossy purple globes of Taggiasca olives, the delicate green of Genovese basil, the plump, sun-ripened tomatoes, and a myriad of other produce that forms the backbone of Ligurian cuisine. The vendors, often multigenerational families, are true connoisseurs of their wares, happy to offer advice on ripeness, preparation, and the best way to enjoy their produce. Their passionate calls and lively banter create an infectious atmosphere, a testament to the enduring human connection at the heart of traditional markets.

Beyond fresh produce, the Mercato Orientale is a treasure trove of artisanal goods. The fishmongers' section is a glistening display of the Mediterranean's bounty, with freshly caught anchovies, sea bream, octopus, and countless other marine delights laid out on beds of ice. The aroma of the sea mingles with the earthy scent of cheeses, cured meats, and freshly baked bread. You'll find exquisite Ligurian cheeses like "prescinseûa," a tangy, creamy cheese essential for many local dishes, alongside a vast selection of salamis, prosciutto, and other cured meats. The bread stalls are equally enticing, offering various focaccia, from the classic plain version glistening with olive oil and sea salt to those topped with onions, olives, or cherry tomatoes.

One of the most delightful aspects of the Mercato Orientale is its dedication to showcasing prepared foods and local specialties. You can find stalls selling freshly made pasta, including the famed "trofie" and "pansoti," often accompanied by generous dollops of vibrant green pesto. The aroma of freshly cooked "farinata," a savory chickpea pancake, wafts through the air, inviting passersby to sample this Genoese staple. Many vendors also offer ready-to-eat Ligurian delicacies, making it an ideal spot for a quick, authentic lunch. You can pick up a slice of "torta pasqualina" (a savory pie with spinach, ricotta, and eggs), a piece of "focaccia di Recco" (a thin, cheesy focaccia), or a selection of fried seafood.

In recent years, the Mercato Orientale has also embraced modernity, with a dedicated food court area on its upper level. Here, contemporary eateries and traditional trattorias coexist, offering a wider range of dining experiences. You can enjoy everything from gourmet sandwiches and craft beers to more elaborate seafood dishes, all while still immersed in the vibrant atmosphere of the market below. This blend of tradition and innovation ensures the Mercato Orientale remains a dynamic and relevant destination for both locals and tourists.

Via XX Settembre

Via XX Settembre, often considered Genoa's most elegant and bustling commercial thoroughfare, serves as the grand artery that leads directly to the heart of the city's culinary scene, including the Mercato Orientale itself. Lined with grand Art Nouveau buildings, ornate porticoes, and a parade of high-end shops, it's a street that embodies the refined spirit of Genoa. While not a market in the traditional sense, Via XX Settembre acts as a major gateway to Genoa's food culture, with numerous cafes, pasticcerie (pastry shops), and specialty food stores peppered along its length and in its immediate vicinity.

The street itself, with its wide pavements and covered walkways, provides a perfect setting for a stroll, perhaps with a traditional Genoese pastry in hand. Here, you can find historic pasticcerie that have been serving delectable treats for generations. Imagine biting into a "sacripantina," a multi-layered cake filled with cream, chocolate, and rum, or enjoying a delicate "canestrello," a shortbread cookie shaped like a flower. These establishments are not just places to buy sweets; they are cultural institutions, that preserve culinary traditions that have been passed down through the ages.

Beyond the pastries, Via XX Settembre is a hub for gourmet food shops. You can discover specialized stores dedicated to olive oil, a cornerstone of Ligurian cuisine, offering a vast selection of extra virgin olive oils from various local producers. There are also shops specializing in pesto, often offering freshly made versions, along with other Ligurian sauces and preserves. Wine shops showcase the region's diverse wines, from the crisp Vermentino to the robust Rossese.

The street's strategic location also means it's surrounded by numerous small trattorias and osterias tucked away in the side streets and alleyways leading off the main thoroughfare. These often unassuming eateries are where you'll find authentic Genoese home cooking: hearty portions of "minestrone alla Genovese," rich stews, and a variety of pasta dishes. Many of these places pride themselves on using fresh ingredients sourced directly from the Mercato Orientale, forging a direct link between the market's bounty and the plates served in local restaurants.

Moreover, Via XX Settembre acts as a vibrant gathering point, often hosting street performers, artists, and occasional food stalls during special events or festivals. This dynamic atmosphere adds another layer to its charm, making it a place where commerce, culture, and cuisine intertwine seamlessly.

In conclusion, Genoa's Mercato Orientale and Via XX Settembre are more than just commercial spaces; they are vital organs of the city's identity. The Mercato Orientale, with its vibrant array of fresh produce, artisanal goods, and prepared delicacies, is a true celebration of Ligurian gastronomy. Via XX Settembre, while a grand commercial avenue, acts as its elegant preamble, inviting visitors to delve deeper into Genoa's rich culinary landscape. Together, they offer an immersive experience that engages all the senses, providing an authentic taste of Genoa's enduring traditions, passionate people, and unparalleled culinary heritage. To truly understand Genoa, one must explore these bustling streets and savor the flavors they so generously offer.

CHAPTER 7: ITINERARY SUGGESTIONS

Whether you're visiting Genoa for a short city break or planning to explore the wider Ligurian region, this chapter offers practical itinerary suggestions tailored to different interests and time frames. From iconic landmarks and scenic promenades to immersive culinary adventures, these itineraries will help you maximize your Genoese experience.

3-Day Highlights Tour for First-Time Visitors

Day 1: Dive into Genoa's Historic Heart

- Start your exploration in Piazza de Ferrari, Genoa's central square, surrounded by ornate buildings and the grand Teatro Carlo Felice. From there, head down Via Garibaldi (Strada Nuova), a UNESCO World Heritage site lined with majestic palazzi like Palazzo Rosso and Palazzo Bianco. These former aristocratic homes now house some of the city's most important art collections.

- Make your way to the Cathedral of San Lorenzo, a striking Gothic-Romanesque structure that anchors Genoa's religious and architectural legacy. Just nearby, explore the Museo Diocesano, filled with religious art and relics.

- In the afternoon, visit the Aquarium of Genoa—Italy's largest—located at the Porto Antico. Afterward, ride the Bigo elevator for panoramic views of the harbor and city skyline. Finish the day with dinner at a seafood restaurant in the Old Port area, where fresh catch and sunset views go hand-in-hand.

Day 2: Fortresses, Views, and Columbus

- Begin your day by visiting Christopher Columbus' House, a modest stone building believed to be his childhood home. Then walk to Porta Soprana, the medieval gate that once guarded the city.

- Take a funicular or bus ride up to Castello d'Albertis, a neo-Gothic castle now housing the Museum of World Cultures. The panoramic views from here are unmatched.

- Later, explore one of Genoa's historic fortresses—Forte Sperone, Forte Diamante, or Forte Begato—depending on your stamina and interest in hiking. These massive 18th- and 19th-century structures are accessible by scenic walks and offer both history and breathtaking vistas.

- Return to the city for dinner at an osteria in the Caruggi (Genoa's maze-like alleyways), where you can sample traditional dishes like trofie al pesto or farinata.

Day 3: Art, Churches, and Modern Vibes

- Spend your last day indulging in Genoa's artistic and spiritual side. Start at Galleria Nazionale di Palazzo Spinola, showcasing a refined collection of Renaissance and Baroque masterpieces. Then head to Chiesa del Gesù and San Matteo, two beautiful examples of Genoese ecclesiastical art.

- Walk along Via XX Settembre for a mix of shopping, local culture, and architecture. Visit the Mercato Orientale, Genoa's vibrant indoor market, where you can try Ligurian specialties or pick up culinary souvenirs.

- End your trip with a walk through the Biosfera and the La Città dei Bambini e dei Ragazzi if you're traveling with kids. Wrap up with dinner at Eataly Genoa, where gourmet regional cuisine meets a sleek, modern setting by the waterfront.

5-Day Genoa and Ligurian Riviera Adventure

Day 1: Genoa Old Town & Waterfront

- Follow the highlights from Day 1 of the 3-day itinerary, covering Via Garibaldi, the cathedral, Porto Antico, the Aquarium, and a scenic elevator ride.

Day 2: Fortresses & Elevated Perspectives

- Choose one or two fortresses for a deeper dive into Genoa's military history. Use the public funicular system for easy access. Later, visit Palazzo Reale, one of the city's grandest noble residences, with its gardens and lavish interiors.

Day 3: Day Trip to Camogli or Nervi

- Take a short train ride to Camogli, a charming fishing village known for its colorful buildings and tranquil beach. Enjoy a seaside lunch and explore Castello della Dragonara. Alternatively, visit Nervi, home to beautiful parks, seaside promenades, and the GAM (Gallery of Modern Art).

Day 4: Day Trip to Cinque Terre or Portofino

- Genoa is a perfect base for exploring Liguria's iconic destinations. Join a guided tour or take the train to Cinque Terre, the string of five cliffside villages famous for their dramatic coastal scenery and pastel-hued homes.

- If you prefer something more refined and leisurely, opt for Portofino, the glamorous resort town nestled in a crescent-shaped bay. Enjoy lunch on the marina and hike up to Castello Brown for panoramic views.

Day 5: Final Touches in Genoa

- Spend your final day visiting the Museo d'Arte Orientale, the Museo di Sant'Agostino, or Villa del Principe, depending on your interest in art and history. Shop for gifts on Via San Luca or at local artisan boutiques. Savor a final Ligurian dinner, perhaps a seafood risotto with a glass of Vermentino wine, and take one last stroll along the harbor under the evening lights.

Foodie's Dream: A Culinary-Focused Itinerary

Day 1: Taste of Tradition

- Begin with a visit to the Mercato Orientale to observe local ingredients, regional produce, and Ligurian herbs in full display. Sample olive oil, sun-dried tomatoes, and cheese. Have lunch at a nearby trattoria with freshly made pansoti (herb-filled ravioli) in walnut sauce.

- In the afternoon, join a pesto-making class, where you'll learn how to prepare Genoa's most famous culinary export using a mortar and pestle. Finish the day with a focaccia tasting—try both sweet and savory varieties at a local panificio.

Day 2: Street Food & Wine

- Explore the caruggi, stopping at family-run eateries and snack bars. Try specialties like farinata (chickpea pancake), frisceu (savory fritters), and torta pasqualina (spinach and egg pie). Visit a wine bar in the evening to sample local Ligurian wines such as Pigato and Rossese, paired with taggiasca olives and anchovies.

Day 3: Seaside Flavors & Gourmet Dining

- Take a culinary walk along the Corso Italia promenade, ending with lunch at a seafood restaurant in Boccadasse, a quaint former fishing village with unforgettable views.

- In the evening, reserve a table at a fine dining establishment like The Cook, a Michelin-starred restaurant offering a modern spin on Genoese classics. Expect dishes like cuttlefish with black ink or Ligurian rabbit with pine nuts and olives.

Day 4: Sweet Side of Genoa

- Dive into Genoa's dessert culture with stops at traditional pastry shops. Sample canestrelli, pandolce, and local gelato infused with basil or citrus. Visit Romanengo, a historic confectioner known for its candied fruit and chocolate.

- Later, take a tour of a historic chocolate workshop or coffee roaster to learn about Genoa's ties to global trade and gourmet goods. End the day with an aperitivo, try vermouth-based cocktails or a refreshing spritz, served with marinated artichokes and bruschetta.

Day 5: Culinary Day Trip or Market Experience

- Take a short trip to Recco, home of the iconic focaccia di Recco, a thin, cheesy delicacy. Enjoy it straight from the oven with local wine. Alternatively, return to Genoa and take a deep dive into the Via XX Settembre food scene, collecting gourmet souvenirs like artisanal pasta, jarred pesto, and Ligurian spices.

- Wrap up with a final meal at a classic osteria, one that's been serving locals for generations, and toast to your gastronomic journey with a shot of limoncello or grappa.

These itinerary suggestions offer something for everyone, whether you're a history buff, a relaxed wanderer, or a devoted foodie. Genoa's rich layers, coastal charm, and flavorful traditions make it a destination worth savoring, day by day, bite by bite, and story by story.

Let your footsteps and taste buds guide you, Genoa is ready to be explored.

CONCLUSION

As you close the final chapter of this travel guide, imagine standing at the edge of Genoa's Porto Antico, with the salty sea breeze brushing your face, a swirl of languages echoing around you, and layers of history stretching behind every stone and facade.

Writing this guide has not only been a labor of love but also a reflection of the many meaningful moments I've had while exploring Genoa and hearing stories from fellow travelers. Genoa is one of those cities that hums beneath the radar of most guidebooks. It doesn't scream for attention, it whispers. But for those who listen, it rewards richly. There's something profoundly authentic about this Ligurian port that draws you in: a city once at the helm of maritime empires, now standing with quiet dignity, offering its soul to the curious.

You've now discovered the city's palaces that glimmer with echoes of aristocracy, the Palazzi dei Rolli, and wandered through ancient alleyways known as caruggi, narrow and shaded, hiding secrets of merchants, poets, and pirates. You've imagined the ornate details inside the Cathedral of San Lorenzo, traced the history of Christopher Columbus through his modest childhood home, and stood beneath the towering Lanterna, Genoa's enduring lighthouse that has guided ships, and perhaps dreams, for centuries.

But Genoa is not just an open-air museum of the past. It pulses with present energy. Through this guide, you've glimpsed the vibrant rebirth of the Old Port, marveled at the futuristic Biosfera, and planned your dive into Genoa's aquarium, the second-largest in Europe. You've mapped out climbs to the scenic forts surrounding the city for panoramic views and considered sipping espresso at Piazza delle Erbe while watching the city go by.

The Genoese people, often described as reserved or pragmatic, open up when you begin to speak their language, sometimes literally, but more often through a mutual appreciation for their city. Ask a barista where to find the best farinata, or a shopkeeper how long their family has been selling cheese and anchovies, and you'll be met with stories that bring the city to life in ways no map can.

And yet, despite its immense charm, Genoa retains a sense of humility. Unlike Italy's more overtly touristic cities, Genoa isn't polished to postcard perfection. It's textured. It's lived-in. There are corners with peeling paint and alleyways that smell of salt, soap, and seaweed. But this, too, is its magic. Genoa doesn't cater to visitors, it welcomes them on its terms.

As a traveler, that's your invitation, not to check off landmarks like items on a list, but to let Genoa change you. Sit on the rocks at Boccadasse and watch the waves slam against the Ligurian shore. Get lost (on purpose) in the twisting lanes of the historic center, and discover that the journey between two points in Genoa is often more rewarding than the destinations themselves.

This guide has aimed to give you the tools, tips, and itineraries to enjoy the best of Genoa, but now the baton is yours. Travel not just with an itinerary, but with curiosity. Let each day unfold with a bit of planning and a lot of openness. Strike up conversations, take detours, and don't worry too much if you don't make it to all 40 attractions listed, sometimes, the best experiences are the ones unplanned.

Whether you're coming to Genoa for a long weekend or making it part of a larger Italian adventure, you'll find that the city lingers in your memory. And perhaps you'll become part of the quiet wave of travelers who return, not just to see what's changed, but to relive what felt right the first time.

In 2025 and 2026, Genoa continues to evolve. From its strides in smart tourism and environmental sustainability to its cultural festivals and a renewed commitment to heritage preservation, the city stands as a bridge between old and new. And you, visitor, wanderer, explorer, are part of that unfolding story.

As I wrap up this guide, I think of the countless messages I've received from fellow travelers over the years. Some were first-timers grateful for an insider's tip, others were seasoned adventurers who, even after multiple visits, still found something new thanks to a page they read here. That's the ultimate reward for any writer in this space, not just to inform, but to inspire.

So let Genoa surprise you. Let it slow you down. Let it feed your soul and challenge your perspective. Let it remind you that beauty often hides in plain sight, waiting not for crowds, but for connection.

Safe travels, and may your time in Genoa be as memorable as the stories you'll take home.

Arrivederci e buon viaggio.

Printed in Dunstable, United Kingdom

66363366R00098